W9-BRY-401

## More Praise for *Humility Is the New Smart*

"As a venture capitalist, I have a front-row seat to the way advances in robotics, sensors, and artificial intelligence are changing the way we work—and it's happening faster than you think. Once again, Ed Hess is out front in his research—this time on the skills and behaviors that will determine whether people and organizations succeed or fail as they adapt to the new reality of working side by side with machines. From CEOs to students, thus is a must-read."
—**Frank H. Foster, Managing Director, Frontier Venture Capital**

"This book was a revelation to me. Who knew that the secret to survival in this intimidating new world of machine intelligence was for us to become more human? In both our business and our private lives, we can choose fear and ego and retreat into ourselves in the face of these challenges, or we can embrace collaboration and positivity instead. Hess and Ludwig show us how to make the life-affirming choice."
—**Jeanne Liedtka, coauthor of *Designing for Growth* and *Solving Problems with Design Thinking***

"An insightful, practical, enriching book for individuals and organizational leaders. NewSmart can be a key to unlocking immense organizational value, one human interaction at a time."
—**Sean Ryan, Senior Vice President, McGraw-Hill Education**

"This book makes the compelling case that true competitive advantage requires human excellence. If you want to be an agile, adaptive, and enabling leader, this book is a must-read."
—**Marvin Riley, President, Fairbanks Morse Engine**

"Original and counterintuitive, this book is essential reading for all who would prepare for the great transformation of employment and work that lies ahead."
—**Rashmi Prasad, Dean, College of Business and Public Policy, University of Alaska Anchorage**

"This compelling book is about how we can succeed in the age of AI—by excelling at what differentiates us as humans. Leaders will have to be good at 'not knowing,' quieting their ego and mastering their fears of looking bad and making mistakes. Instead of managing others, leaders will have to manage themselves to enable others."
—**Peter Rodriguez, Dean, Jones Graduate School of Business, Rice University**

"Hess and Ludwig offer revolutionary approaches to self-management along with innovative and insightful leadership platforms for the Smart Machine Age. A powerful book!"
—**Jeanette K. Winters, Senior Vice President and Chief Human Resource Officer, Igloo Products Corporation**

"Outstanding book with rock-solid arguments about why doing a 'good job' will no longer be good enough in a smart machine world and how NewSmart beliefs and behaviors can help humankind master this challenge."
**—Kurt D. Bettenhausen, Chair, Digital Transformation Group, VDI, Germany**

"How must our notions about individual and organizational excellence adapt to the Smart Machine Age? Hess and Ludwig offer insights that are perceptive, provocative, and powerful! Their ideas can help your organization and you adapt to the coming transformations spurred by big data, deep learning, artificial intelligence, and automation."
**—Robert F. Bruner, University Professor, University of Virginia**

"*Humility Is the New Smart* is a must-read for business and political leaders, parents, teachers, and everyone interested in understanding the challenges and opportunities of the coming Smart Machine Age. The explanation of humility—its philosophical meaning and application to leadership—is the best I've ever read."
**—Fernando Mercé, President, Latin America and Caribbean, Nestlé Purina**

"Hess and Ludwig crush it in *Humility Is the New Smart*. They introduce the compelling concept of NewSmart, which will help learners successfully navigate the coming Smart Machine Age. They want our young people to be adaptive lifelong learners, and embracing NewSmart is a path to learning for the future, not our past."
**—Dr. Pamela R. Moran, Superintendent, Albemarle County Public Schools, Virginia**

"This fascinating examination of what it will take to thrive in the Smart Machine Age offers a compelling and profoundly humane manual on how to achieve our highest expressions of excellence, in business and in all our interactions."
**—Ming-Jer Chen, former President, Academy of Management, and Professor, Darden School of Business, University of Virginia**

"*Humility Is the New Smart* provides a provocative view of the kinds of individual skills necessary to succeed in the future. Through their exhaustive interdisciplinary research, the authors give us practical advice on how we can best prepare ourselves to excel in the Smart Machine Age."
**—Wally Walker, founder of Hana Road Capital and former CEO, Seattle Supersonics**

"As a father and the leader of a school responsible for preparing students for their future, I embraced the authors' premise that we need to change our mindsets, skills, and behaviors for a more dynamic technology-based world. They provide compelling research and very practical tools to help us on our journey. Listen well—our futures and our children's futures depend on it."
**—G. Thomas Battle, Jr., Headmaster, Virginia Episcopal School**

# Humility
## Is the
# New Smart

# Humility
## Is the
# New Smart

**Rethinking Human Excellence
in the Smart Machine Age**

Edward D. Hess
Katherine Ludwig

BK·
Berrett–Koehler Publishers, Inc.
*a BK Business book*

**Berrett-Koehler Publishers, Inc.**
1333 Broadway, Suite 1000
Oakland, CA 94612-1921
Tel: (510) 817-2277      Fax: (510) 817-2278      www.bkconnection.com

Ordering Information
Quantity sales. Special discounts are available on quantity purchases by corporations, associations, and others. For details, contact the "Special Sales Department" at the Berrett-Koehler address above.
**Individual sales.** Berrett-Koehler publications are available through most bookstores. They can also be ordered directly from Berrett-Koehler: Tel: (800) 929-2929; Fax: (802) 864-7626; www.bkconnection.com
**Orders for college textbook/course adoption use.** Please contact Berrett-Koehler: Tel: (800) 929-2929; Fax: (802) 864-7626.

Distributed to the U.S. trade and internationally by Penguin Random House Publisher Services.

Berrett-Koehler and the BK logo are registered trademarks of Berrett-Koehler Publishers, Inc.

Printed in the United States of America

Berrett-Koehler books are printed on long-lasting acid-free paper. When it is available, we choose paper that has been manufactured by environmentally responsible processes. These may include using trees grown in sustainable forests, incorporating recycled paper, minimizing chlorine in bleaching, or recycling the energy produced at the paper mill.

Library of Congress Cataloging-in-Publication Data
Names: Hess, Edward D., author. | Ludwig, Katherine, author.
Title: Humility is the new smart : rethinking human excellence in the smart machine age / by Edward D. Hess and Katherine Ludwig.
Description: First Edition. | Oakland : Berrett-Koehler Publishers, 2017. | Includes bibliographical references and index.
Identifiers: LCCN 2016039284 | ISBN 9781626568754 (hardcover)
Subjects: LCSH: Intellect. | Human behavior. | Human-computer interaction. | Artificial intelligence. | Machine-to-machine communications.
Classification: LCC BF431 .H435 2017 | DDC 650.1—dc23
LC record available at https://lccn.loc.gov/2016039284

First Edition
21  20  19  18          10  9  8  7  6  5  4  3

Project management, design, and composition by Steven Hiatt, Hiatt & Dragon, San Francisco
Copyeditor: Paula Dragosh    Proofreader: Tom Hassett    Indexer: Theresa Duran    Cover designer: Kirk DouPonce, DogEared Design

To Lyle E. Bourne Jr., Kim Cameron, Arthur W. Combs,
Jane E. Dutton, Linda Elder, Barbara L. Fredrickson,
Sidney M. Jourard, Gary Klein, and Richard Paul,
whose work inspired me.
*– EH*

To my family, for their humbling support and encouragement.
*– KL*

# Contents

Introduction: Why You Should Read This Book     1

### Part 1 A New Mental Model for the Smart Machine Age

1   The Smart Machine Age: A New Game Requires New Rules     15

2   NewSmart: A New Definition of "Smart"     35

3   Humility: The Gateway to Human Excellence in the SMA     59

### Part 2 NewSmart Behaviors

4   Quieting Ego     79

5   Managing Self: Thinking and Emotions     95

6   Reflective Listening     115

7   Otherness: Emotionally Connecting and Relating to Others     123

8   Your NewSmart Behaviors Assessment Tool     133

### Part 3 The NewSmart Organization

9   Leading a NewSmart Organization     153

Your NewSmart Organizational Assessment Tool     183

Epilogue: Our Invitation to You     187

Notes     189

Recommended Reading     201

Acknowledgments     205

Index     207

About the Authors     212

# Introduction

# Why You Should Read This Book

Society is on the leading edge of a technology tsunami. Advances in artificial intelligence, the Internet of Things, virtual reality, robotics, nanotechnology, deep learning, mapping the human brain, and biomedical, genetic, and cyborg engineering will revolutionize how most of us live and work. Technology will be able to learn, as well as teach and program itself. We call this next big step the Smart Machine Age, or SMA.

The SMA has the potential to be as disruptive and transformative for us as the Agricultural Age and Industrial Revolution were for our ancestors. In the last few decades, the American worker has been outsourced, offshored, and automated on many factory floors and in many routine tasks. Up next is a broader and more encompassing automation that will likely affect many more workers, including many professionals. This new reality should cause many of us to ask:

Could a robot or smart machine replace me?
How can I thrive in this new era?
What can I do now to start preparing for the SMA?

What could this mean for my career plans? Will I have meaningful work?

What do my children need to do to begin preparing for this new age?

## The Smart Machine Age Is Coming Soon

The impact of technology on our economy and our lives is nothing new.[1] Technology has driven vast improvements in productivity while allowing businesses to maintain or lower labor costs and has put GDP and national income mostly on an upward trajectory since World War II. However, the median income of most workers has increased little since 1979 and has been on the decrease since 1999.[2] Wages for average production and nonsupervisory workers as of 2013 were 13 percent less than in 1973 (adjusted for inflation), even though productivity grew 107 percent and the costs of housing, education, and health care rose dramatically.[3] As a result, income inequality is at levels not seen since 1929.[4] Many people are working as hard as ever for less pay, and advancing technologies are at least partly to blame.

Moreover, for the last few years, the percentage of "contingent workers," including part-time and temporary workers and independent contractors, has risen and now makes up a whopping 40 percent of the workforce, according to an April 2015 report of the US Government Accountability Office.[5] While automation has been happening for decades, up until now robots have been, well, robotic: good at doing what they're told in explicit terms by direct or indirect (that is, remote) human manipulation. What is and will be different soon is that machines are getting smarter by the day and even now are able to tackle both cognitive and nonroutine manual tasks previously thought the exclusive purview of humans. Technology is even beginning to replace knowledge workers, people who have believed that their professions were immune to automation, including accountants, business managers, doctors, lawyers, journalists, researchers, architects, higher-education teachers, and consultants. **Smart technologies will become ubiquitous, invading and changing many aspects of our professional and personal lives and in many ways challenging our fundamental beliefs about success, opportunity, and the American Dream.**

## What Is the Likely Impact?

The best research to date from Oxford University and the Bank of England indicates a high probability that technology will replace 47 percent of US jobs or displace as many as eighty million US workers within the next ten to twenty years.[6] The consensus view is that humans will be needed to perform those skills that either complement technology or constitute what machines can't yet do well, and that list includes **critical thinking, innovative thinking, creativity,** and the kind of **high emotional engagement with others** that fosters relationship building and collaboration. We call these SMA Skills.

Other experts—whom we call the "techno-optimists"—are predicting that technology will produce plenty of new jobs to replace those lost because that's what happened in the Industrial Revolution. In other words, they believe that history will repeat itself. We're skeptical of that view for two reasons. First, that prediction ignores the widespread human havoc created by the Industrial Revolution, which for example in England lasted more than sixty years before society adjusted. Second, a big question is whether technology will produce *tens of mil-*

*lions* of new jobs that technology itself won't be able to do.

**Our prediction, based on the data, is that this upheaval in the number and types of available jobs and required skills will turn our lives and our children's lives upside down.** The jobs available for humans will require high-level thinking, creativity, and high emotional intelligence. Those skills present a challenge for us, because while they're uniquely human, they run counter to human nature—which is generally reflexive both cognitively and emotionally—and the manner in which we've been trained, educated, and nurtured.

As we explain in more detail in chapter 1, we humans tend not to be good critical or innovative thinkers, and we tend to engage in fast thinking tainted by cognitive biases. Our emotions are inextricably intertwined with cognition, and depending on whether and how we manage them, these emotions can either enhance or undermine our behavior, thinking, and decision making.[7] We tend to "defend, deny, and deflect" when confronted with information that challenges our beliefs. Our nature can cause us to think and behave in ways that protect our egos, and we usually listen to confirm, not to learn. Our evolutionary fight-flee-or-freeze response is triggered by fears of failure and embarrassment that interfere with our abilities to engage in creativity, critical and innovative thinking, and emotional engagement with others.[8]

All the above cognitive and emotional challenges can diminish the quality of our thinking and our ability to collaborate with others. We know from the science that very few of us can think creatively, critically, or innovatively at the highest levels by ourselves. We need the help of others to do that. The SMA Skills are "team activities." In addition, from a nurture viewpoint, our US culture (this book is written from a US perspective) encourages self-centered individualism and thus inhibits the more outward-focused mindsets and behaviors needed to do the kind of high-order thinking and emotional engagement with others that will be the key employable skills in the SMA.

These are our challenges. We humans have to overcome our inhibiting cultural mindsets, our reflexive cognitive and emotional ways, and what the social psychologist Barbara Fredrickson calls our "cocoon of self-absorption"[9] in order to compete effectively and complement smart machines, which will have no biases (unless through human design), no egos, no emotional defensiveness, and no fears of making mistakes or looking stupid or not being liked. The purpose of this book is to propose how we can become much better thinkers, listeners, relators, and collaborators and overcome our culture of obsessive individualism in order to thrive in the SMA. Our book is a story of how to strive for human excellence—from individual, team, and organizational viewpoints.

### What Can We Do?

We'll have to change the behaviors that inhibit our abilities to excel at SMA Skills. Based on our research into the science of critical thinking, innovative thinking, creativity, and emotional and social intelligence, and from Ed's fieldwork inside high-performance learning organizations, we believe that there are four fundamental behaviors that will help us overcome our nature and nurture limitations: **Quieting Ego, Managing Self** (one's thinking and emotions), **Reflective Listening,** and **Otherness** (emotionally connecting and relating to others).

For most of us, these behaviors require that we radically change how we negotiate the world. Research shows that people are more inclined to change their behavior if they first change their personal beliefs—their "mental models"—in a manner that supports the desired behaviors. That requires us to fundamentally change our story about what it means to be smart in the SMA. **The first hero in our story is NewSmart. It's a new definition of what it means to be "smart" in our society and what it takes to succeed in a world in which technology will in many ways be smarter than we are.**

## NewSmart

Today the dominant definition of "smart" is quantity based. It means that I'm smarter than you if I know more than you. To determine that, we typically see which one of us makes the fewest mistakes or gets the highest test scores. This definition is partly a legacy of the Industrial Revolution's need for mass education of workers who could perform the required repetitive manual tasks in factories without making mistakes. Today it's a consequence of a knowledge-based economy where "knowing more" is rewarded.

In the SMA, that definition of smart that we call Old Smart won't work. It'll be impossible for humans to know more content than a smart machine. Such machines will be able to process, remember, recall, pattern match, find variances, and synthesize more data faster and more accurately than any human. Humans will never outsmart smart machines if quantity of knowledge is the standard. Additionally, Old Smart breeds intolerance of mistakes and failure, which are required for the kind of iterative learning that underlies innovation, scientific discovery, entrepreneurship, and creativity. In the SMA, Old Smart will become the new "stupid."

NewSmart is a new definition of human smart that reflects the increasing cognitive capabilities of smart machines and is measured not by *quantity*—how much you know—but by the *quality* of your thinking, learning, and emotionally engaging with others. NewSmart is not about always being right, being perfect, and knowing more than others.

**To be NewSmart is to excel at the highest level of thinking, learning, and emotionally engaging with others that one is capable of doing.**

In chapter 2, we discuss how we came to our definition of NewSmart and the underlying ideas about what quality thinking entails. We introduce the work of critical thinking experts and share what we've learned from Ray Dalio, the founder of Bridgewater Associates—the largest and one of the most successful hedge funds in the world—and from Ed Catmull, a founder of the highly creative and innovative Pixar Animation Studios. We explain how and why in the SMA we must think more like scientists, embrace the magnitude of our ignorance, collaborate with others, and learn from our mistakes and failures.

NewSmart leads us to our second hero: Humility. Why humility? Because we know from the scientific research that two big inhibitors of quality thinking, learning, and emotionally engaging with others are our *ego* and our *fears*. Studies of high-performance learning organizations confirmed these findings. To mitigate ego and fear and excel at the highest levels of human thinking and emotional engagement requires a new mindset that embraces humility.

## Humility

What do we mean by Humility? We do *not* mean its common connotation in US culture: being meek or being subdued or thinking that you're not a worthy person. Our definition is derived from psychological science, Western critical thinking philosophy, and Eastern philosophy. Our definition of humility, which we refer to throughout this book with a capital H, means **a mindset about oneself that is open-minded, self-accurate, and "not all about me," and that enables one to embrace the world as it "is" in the pursuit of human excellence.** We believe that our definition of Humility is the gateway to human excellence in the SMA because it enables the behaviors that underlie the high performance of SMA Skills. As we explain further in chapter 3, Humility is a mindset that results in not being so self-centered, ego defensive, self-enhancing, self-promotional, and closed-minded—all of which the science of learning and cognition shows inhibit excellence at higher-order thinking and emotionally engaging with others.

We recognize that Humility may be a hard concept for some successful people to buy into initially because they'll believe that it runs counter to their being perceived as strong, smart, and confident. That view is changing in our society: the exemplar organizations and leaders we discuss in this book already embrace Humility, including Google, Pixar, Bridgewater Associates, Intuit, and the US Navy SEALs.

Perhaps some of you are saying to yourself: I already am a good thinker. I am a good listener. I do relate well to other people. I'm not self-centered. We thought that, too, seven years ago (and we had achieved success to prove it). But we were wrong. We were good enough, but good enough won't cut it anymore. In the SMA, the highest levels of thinking, listening, relating, and collaborating with others will be the pathways to success for many of us and our children. And reaching that high level requires that we behave in ways that are more likely to drive those results. Our story about SMA success and excellence has two heroes—NewSmart and Humility—and a desired ending: the ability to excel at the four SMA Skills. That leads us to the final part of our story: how "to do" the four fundamental behaviors that are required in order to excel at the SMA Skills. We call those four behaviors the NewSmart Behaviors.

### The NewSmart Behaviors

In chapters 4 through 7, we explain why Quieting Ego, Managing Self (one's thinking and emotions), Reflective Listening, and Otherness (emotionally connecting and relating to others) are necessary for excelling at the SMA Skills, and we provide guidance on how to adopt those behaviors and how to improve them based on research, our work with senior managers and leaders, and our own experiences. Most people we have worked with reflexively respond to these behaviors by saying, "I am good at that." But after learning about the various sub-behaviors that underlie and define those main behaviors, nearly everyone comes to the same conclusions that we came to: we can take our thinking, listening, managing self, and emotionally engaging "games" to a much higher level. That's what we all must do.

This is a "how to" book, because knowing what to do is not enough—we need to actually do it and do it excellently and consistently. We must make the choice to deliberately practice the NewSmart Behaviors. Just like world-class athletes, dancers, and musicians train, most of us will have to train our cognitive, emotional, and self-management "muscles" to excel at the NewSmart Behaviors that underlie the thinking and emotionally engaging skills that can separate us from smart machines.

To help you do that, you'll have the opportunity in chapter 8 to use a NewSmart Behaviors Assessment Tool to evaluate the level at which you currently engage in the NewSmart Behaviors and where you have room for improvement. Ed developed this tool in his work with more than a thousand managers and leaders over the last few years. Every one of those senior managers and leaders came to the same conclusions we did after focusing on what sub-behaviors are necessary to excel at the four NewSmart Behaviors—we need to improve. After the assessment, you'll find guidance on how to create your own NewSmart Behaviors Personal Improvement Plan based on the leading science of how best to train, learn, and master new skills through deliberate practice. Our goal is to help you start on your SMA journey to personal excellence with an actionable and measurable behavioral improvement plan.

## Leading a NewSmart Organization

In chapter 9 we switch our focus from the individual to the team and organization. Although technology will in many cases reduce the size of the human workforce, we believe that it will also humanize most business organizations. Why? Because in the SMA, humans will be needed to do the highest levels of thinking and emotional engagement, and organizations will have to create the right environment that enables and promotes those behaviors. That requires a positive, people-centric, humanistic work environment. Ironically, then, technology will likely both dehumanize and humanize organizations.

Leading an organization that can remain competitive in the SMA requires implementing a culture and processes designed to embrace NewSmart, cultivate Humility, and encourage the NewSmart Behaviors in order to develop and excel at the human capabilities needed to achieve the organizational mission. **This environment must be designed to reduce the two biggest human learning inhibitors—ego and fear. Three psychological concepts form the foundation of such an environment: Positivity, Self-Determination Theory, and Psychological Safety.** The science of learning and examples from the studies of high-performance learning organizations offer a research-based roadmap to begin to lead a NewSmart organization.

## Our Learning Journey

This book has been a work-in-progress for several years. Our research has taken us across many fields—philosophy, psychology, behavioral economics, education, the basic hard sciences, sociology, history, law, engineering, business, arts, evolutionary biology, and anthropology. We devoured over six hundred leading academic articles and over one hundred leading books and conducted field research with individuals and organizations on the cutting edge of human development of the SMA Skills. At the end of the book you'll find key references and a recommended reading list for additional information.

Our research has been motivated by imagination and concern—imagining what our world and our children's and grandchildren's worlds may look like in the SMA and concern about how they and our society will adapt to the coming technology revolution. And we have been motivated by our personal concern about how we, just like you, stay relevant in the SMA. From our research, we concluded that the magnitude of the upcoming changes requires a new story of what human success looks like when we're working side by side with machines that are in many ways much smarter than us. And that new story needs to help us behave in ways that increase our chances of staying relevant and having meaningful work in the SMA.

None of us wants to be left behind or, as Jerry Kaplan, a computer scientist and Silicon Valley entrepreneur, warns in *Humans Need Not Apply*, the last human left to turn off the lights. (Actually, no worries, says Kaplan: "They can turn themselves off."[10])

This book is a call to action for anyone seventeen or older. The smart machines are coming, and we need to get ready! We invite you to read on and learn how to think, listen, relate, and collaborate better in order to reach your highest potential at work and in life. We invite you to join us in pursuing human excellence in the SMA.

# Part I

# A New Mental Model
# for the Smart Machine Age

# I

# The Smart Machine Age:
# A New Game Requires New Rules

> We can be humble and live a good life with the aid
> of the machines or we can be arrogant and die.
> —*Norbert Wiener*

Norbert Wiener, an MIT mathematics professor and computer science pioneer, wrote those words in 1948 in a recently discovered unpublished essay for the *New York Times*. He literally meant them as an apocryphal warning about the dangers to humanity of uncontrolled advances in automation and artificial intelligence. For decades, such dire predictions remained on the fringe of societal concerns and relevant only to science fiction fans. The technologies that were only a gleam in Wiener's eye, however, have finally come to fruition.

Smart machines are becoming autonomous and able to tackle nonroutine cognitive tasks previously thought the exclusive purview of people. Machines are gaining natural language capabilities, voice and facial recognition, and the ability to draft sports columns and analyze due diligence documents better and faster than many human reporters or lawyers. Thanks to advances in automated perception, sensors, and robotics, machines are now able to handle what had previously prevented them from tackling nonroutine manual jobs as well, such as driving cars, picking out products from warehouse shelves, and sorting mail. High-functioning humanoid robots can now be seen on hospital floors and in hotels, restaurants, museums, and shopping malls. They aren't just flipping burgers behind the scenes: they're interacting with patrons and patients—like "Connie," the robot concierge Hilton began rolling out in 2016 in lobbies across the country in partnership with IBM Watson.

With respect to nonroutine cognitive jobs, using automated tools and algorithms, machines can now handle data analytics, pattern recognition, and deductive reasoning. Machines are becoming better than a roomful of Wharton graduates at devising portfolio investment theory for hedge funds and better than a team of Sloan-Kettering doctors at diagnosing illnesses.[1] With investments from companies like Google, implantable biometric sensors will soon allow us to monitor our own health.[2] Facial expression analysis software will detect the emotions and engagement of others better than our own minds.[3] A group of researchers from MIT and the Masdar Institute, who conducted the first quantitative study of skill content changes in occupations between 2006 and 2014, concluded, "For any given skill one can think of, some computer scientist somewhere may already be trying to develop an algorithm to do it."[4]

Combining the development of artificial neural codes and networks that model the human brain with access to Big Data, programmers can give machines the ability to process information and learn on a level that rivals and may soon exceed that of the human race.

Machines quite literally are now beating us at our own games. In March 2016 in what many artificial intelligence (AI) experts touted as the match of the century, AlphaGo—a computer program developed by Google's DeepMind AI company—defeated South Korean Go master Lee Se-dol four matches to one in the ancient Chinese strategy game. Almost twenty years after IBM's supercomputer DeepBlue bested the chess champion Gary Kasparov, AlphaGo's victory still surprised many experts who predicted that it would take at least another decade to develop a computer program with the ability to outwit and out-strategize a Go master in arguably the most complicated human board game ever invented. The CEO of DeepMind, Demis Hassabis, said that algorithms used for AlphaGo "one day can be used in all sorts of problems, from health care to science."[5]

Plenty of today's technology experts, from Silicon Valley entrepreneurs to current MIT and University of Oxford academics, have sounded alarms about the potentially devastating impacts to our economy and society because of such recent and imminent technology advances.[6] We repeat Wiener's warning here, however, not because we believe that the robot apocalypse is around the corner but because we believe that it's crucial to our relevancy as human workers and the vitality of the organizations for which we work that we pause and acknowledge the drastic changes coming and prepare ourselves to not only survive but to thrive.

We believe that there's a path to successfully navigating these strange new highly automated waters, but many of us will have to fundamentally change our views of what it means for humans to be "smart" and what it takes for humans to succeed and reach their fullest potential. To do otherwise—to ignore the impact and fail to prepare for what's to come—would indeed be a foolhardy exercise in human arrogance.

## Smart Machines and a New Era

There's a growing consensus among most computer science experts, economists, and business leaders that smart machines—whether humanoid robots or invisible networked connections—that can learn, think, and perform both manual and cognitive tasks in most cases better than their human counterparts could be the biggest game changer both personally and organizationally since the Industrial Revolution. It's likely that the business, education, and leadership models created for the Industrial Revolution could become obsolete. Technological and scientific advances in artificial intelligence, the Internet of Things, virtual reality, robotics, nanotechnology, deep learning, mapping the human brain, and biomedical, genetic, and cyborg engineering could fundamentally change how all of us—from laborers to knowledge workers—live and find livelihood.

Technology that can learn and even program itself will become ubiquitous in homes, factories, and offices and soon displace even the highly educated people who have thought that their professions are immune to the risks of automation, including accountants, business managers, doctors, lawyers, journalists, researchers, architects, higher-education teachers, and consultants. Artificial intelligence—deep learning or machine learning—will be especially transformative in this regard. Speaking at a technology industry conference in May 2016, Jeff Bezos, the founder of Amazon, stated, "It's probably hard to overstate how big of an impact it's going to have on society over the next 20 years."[7]

Andrew Ng, an associate professor of computer science at Stanford University, a chief scientist at Baidu, and chairman and cofounder of Coursera, recently told the *Wall Street Journal*: "The age of intelligent machines will see huge numbers of individuals unable to work, unable to earn, unable to pay taxes. Those workers will need to be retrained—or risk being left out in the cold. We could face labor displacement of a magnitude we haven't seen since the 1930s."[8]

Similarly, Kevin Kelly, co-founder of *Wired* magazine, says in his new book *The Inevitable: Understanding the 12 Technological Forces That Will Shape Our Future*: "It is hard to imagine anything that would 'change everything' as much as cheap, powerful, ubiquitous artificial intelligence.... The advantages gained from cognifying inert things would be hundreds of times more disruptive to our lives than the transformations gained by industrialization."[9]

In the next two decades, technological advances could displace as many as eighty million US workers, according to the chief economist of the Bank of England,[10] or 47 percent of the US workforce, based on a 2013 study by leading researchers at Oxford University.[11] According to a study by McKinsey & Company, by adapting technologies already demonstrated as of 2015, as many as 45 percent of the job tasks US workers are currently paid to do could be automated. Not even the most highly skilled or highly paid are safe. McKinsey also estimated that current technology could be adapted to replace at least 20 percent of a CEO's work activities.

The result is that no longer will human scale be necessary for value creation in most fields. Without question, technology will transform how most businesses operate and are staffed in terms of both numbers and job requirements and skills.

Routine jobs in hierarchical organizations—both those requiring manual and those requiring cognitive skills—will rapidly disappear. Most businesses in the near future will be staffed by some combination of smart robots, smart machines, and humans, and the job and skill requirements for each will be in flux.

In addition, the kind of long-term employment at stable organizations that characterized previous generations will be rare. The percentage of "contingent workers," including part-time, temporary, and independent contractors, has been on the rise and recently made up a whopping 40 percent of the workforce, according to an April 2015 report of the US Government Accountability Office.[12] Another recent study predicted that by 2020, over half of the country's workforce will be consultants, freelancers, and independent contractors, cobbling together their own gigs.[13]

Martin Ford, a Silicon Valley entrepreneur and the author of *Rise of the Robots: Technology and the Threat of a Jobless Future*, recently argued that "emerging industries will rarely, if ever, be highly labor-intensive"; rather, they'll be more like YouTube and Instagram, "where we've come to expect tiny work forces and huge valuations and revenues."[14] Similarly, Tony Wagner argues: "While the Intels, IBMs, and Genentechs of the last century employed hundreds of thousands (the majority of whom were low- and middle-skilled workers), the Googles, Facebooks, and Twitters of the 21st century will employ an order of magnitude fewer employees. Almost all of them will be creative problem-solvers."[15] Howard Gardner made a similar statement: "The future belongs to those organizations, as well as those individuals that have made an active lifelong commitment to learning."[16]

In the age of these smart machines—what we're calling the Smart Machine Age or SMA—operational excellence may well become almost totally technology-driven, making human innovation the key to value creation. Organizations will need their people to be hyperlearners who can adapt to rapidly changing environments. These needs are unlike what was required in the command-and-control-style organizations of the Industrial Age or more recently with respect to the repetitive and routine nature of knowledge work. Agility, adaptability, and responsiveness also will be required for most, and thus organizational efficiency will be necessary but no longer sufficient. The type of human learning that will be required is continuous and iterative learning, where one's beliefs are constantly stress-tested against changing phenomena and adapted to better reflect reality. Those human processes are not efficient. In fact, they are hard and emotionally messy.

## What's Left for Humans to Do?

Humans can no longer add value by merely accumulating or analyzing knowledge. The creation of new knowledge is increasing exponentially, and it's now believed that most knowledge has a less than three-year shelf life. What you think you "know" is so quickly out of date that you must continually update your learning. Moreover, it'll be impossible for humans to know more facts or concepts than a smart machine or be able to process, remember, recall, pattern match, and synthesize more data faster or more accurately than smart machines such as Google's AlphaGo and IBM's *Jeopardy!*-winning Watson.

Instead, to be marketable and stay relevant in the SMA, humans will need to excel at the kinds of jobs and skills that either complement technology or are those that technology cannot do well—at least not yet. That list includes **critical thinking**, innovative thinking, creativity, and **high emotional engagement with others** that fosters relationship building and collaboration. Collectively we refer to these as the SMA Skills. (Note that by creativity we mean to refer to the original expression of ideas and thoughts, including through art and otherwise. By innovation, we mean to refer to the commercialization of new ideas, methods, or things.)

Other jobs that will remain in the near future are those manual jobs requiring customized tasks and physical dexterity, but here we're focusing on the cognitive skills remaining for the majority of us who consider ourselves knowledge workers. Regardless of job or position, most of us will have to think and behave more like scientists, entrepreneurs, and artists and better engage socially and emotionally with others. The SMA Skills amount to our summary of the conclusions drawn by leading business and education leaders, economists, and researchers at MIT, Oxford, McKinsey & Company, the World Economic Forum, and the National Educational Association, among many other experts on the most important human skills in the twenty-first century.[17]

The purpose of this book, however, is not to justify or debate the primacy of the four SMA Skills or to address, for example, when and if computers will ever achieve a human level of creativity. Much has already been written about the need to better incorporate twenty-first-century skills into primary and secondary education and job training programs and to close the skills gap to maintain US competitiveness in the global economy. Our purpose is to focus on how we humans can excel at those skills and thrive in the SMA. Unfortunately, for reasons of both nature and nurture, most of us face challenges in that regard.

### Why SMA Skills Are So Hard for Humans

While the SMA Skills are what humans increasingly will need to master to stay relevant, they're far from easy to execute well. We need to understand that many of today's business leaders and managers have not been trained to develop or cultivate critical and innovative thinking, creativity, and high emotional engagement with others. They were raised, educated, and trained instead in an era when higher-order thinking and emotional skills were not deemed essential for the majority of workers. Most of today's adults have had no formal training in how to think, how to listen, how to learn and experiment through inquiry, how to emotionally engage, how to manage emotions, how to collaborate, or how to embrace mistakes as learning opportunities. This is because US society (note that we're addressing these issues from the perspective of Western and particularly US culture) favors high grades over mastery, aggressiveness and competitiveness, and the avoidance of failure at all costs—all of which hinder thinking, creating, relating, and learning at our best.

### Our humanness is a blessing and a curse

We can all probably agree that SMA Skills constitute what humans can do at their best and brightest. When we're functioning at our highest level, we're able to think critically and innovatively, be creative, and relate socially and emotionally to and collaborate with others. That's our human advantage over the "bots" and algorithms. The good news is that recent research in neuroscience and cognitive, social, and educational psychology has begun to show us the environments, mindsets, and behaviors most conducive to enabling this kind of higher-order thinking, relating, and creating. The bad news is that most of us are really bad at creating those environments and embodying those underlying mindsets and behaviors because of both human nature and how we've been nurtured, which together generate two big inhibitors to learning and thinking: a preoccupation with protecting our own egos and a fear of failing and looking bad.

Let's take critical thinking, for instance. The *Oxford English Dictionary* defines it as "the objective analysis and evaluation of an issue in order to form a judgment." The key word is *objective*, and it's this objectivity that underlies the cognitive psychologist Daniel Willingham's more elaborate definition of critical thinking: "seeing both sides of an issue, being open to new evidence that disconfirms your ideas, reasoning dispassionately, demanding that claims be backed by evidence, deducing and inferring conclusions from available facts, solving problems, and so forth."[18]

Critical thinking is different from our usual way of thinking precisely because being "objective" is so difficult to do. You may believe that you're thinking critically much of the time, but chances are you aren't doing it as well as you think you are, as well as you could, or as well as increasingly you'll need to. Scientific research has revealed just how hard it can be for humans to think and behave at their best in our modern world because of basic human biology and evolution. Our strong inclination is to be confirmation-biased and emotionally defensive thinkers.

As Daniel Kahneman, a psychologist and Nobel Laureate, explains in his treatise *Thinking, Fast and Slow*, we've evolved to have two systems of thinking. System 1 is fast, automatic, and subconscious—we can think of this as our intuition, which is not flying by the seat of our pants necessarily but relying on the internal beliefs, ideas, and perceptions that we consciously or unconsciously form from our experiences. Psychologists refer to this bundle of beliefs, ideas, and perceptions as our "mental models." They enable us to pattern match and make connections and associations that are quick and often subconscious. System 2 is our slow, deliberate, and effortful process of reasoning—it's closer to critical-type thinking, but not always quite there, as we'll explain further.

### Our reactivity

System 1 was the first to develop in our evolutionary biology, and you can see why—there's no need to pause to deliberate about what to do when you hear the telltale signs of a predator approaching. Our minds developed several cognitive biases and heuristics as shortcuts to help us survive. In many cases our cognitive biases are wrong, however, and compromise our thinking and decisions. But when you're in actual survival mode—Is that woolly mammoth about to charge?—you're better safe than sorry. Not so in our modern world, where our cognitive biases have us often making faulty judgments based on, for example, stereotypes and groupthink.

As Kahneman explains, our minds are limited by "excessive confidence in what we believe we know, and our apparent inability to acknowledge the full extent of our ignorance."[19] "We can be blind to the obvious," he says, and also "blind to our blindness."[20] Also, "our memories are heavily influenced by ease of recall; our emotions (likes and dislikes); and our inherent comfort with coherence that leads to overconfidence."[21]

The other important point to note when considering these two systems is that even when we set out to be more deliberate and thoughtful in our decision making and use System 2, our thinking is still often "biased, distorted, partial, uninformed, or downright prejudiced," as Richard Paul and Linda Elder explain on their Critical Thinking Community website. Our thinking even when deliberate is also always influenced by our subconscious perceptions of reality that are colored not only by implicit biases but by our beliefs, assumptions, and experiences about the world that can inhibit us from seeing other sides of an issue or thinking outside the box.

Another problem is that we're bad at recognizing when our own thinking is faulty because, as Kahneman states, "laziness is built deep into our nature" and "it is much easier, as well as far more enjoyable, to identify and label the mistakes of others than to recognize our own."[22] We tend to brush off those who do recognize our biases and critique our thinking or beliefs, because, as another Nobel Laureate, Herbert Simon, once said, "People who agree with you are apt to seem a little more intelligent than those who don't."[23] Thus it's clear that to effectively think in ways that smart machines can't think, we need to acknowledge that we need the help of others to open our eyes to disconfirming data and different perspectives, which is why relationship building with other people will be even more important in the SMA.

*Our irrationality*
Another crucial point to understand about human thinking is that reason cannot be separated from emotional processes, and thus rationality is a myth. Psychologists and neuroscientists have made tremendous discoveries in the last two decades

that confirm that cognitive and emotional processes are inextricably intertwined in our minds and that learning, attention, memory, and decision making are profoundly affected by emotion and in fact subsumed within the processes of emotion. This is at odds with the Descartian belief in rationalism so preeminent in our Western learning traditions.[24]

Ignoring emotions can be as debilitating as allowing excessive emotions to take over. Emotions inform, mediate, and sometimes cloud our cognitive processing, learning, and social interactions. This isn't a flaw; it's just a fact. Research has shown that positive emotions and mood are associated with broader attention and more expansive and flexible thinking, while negative emotions such as stress, anger, anxiety, or defensiveness can impede decision making and problem solving.[25]

The reality of this situation—the two systems of thinking, the subconscious biases, the importance of other people in helping us recognize those biases, and the interconnection of cognition and emotional processes—is why to do our best, most high-level, critical thinking, we need to first acknowledge our limitations and then slow down, be mindful, and learn to manage our thinking processes, our emotions, and our thinking behaviors to understand and account for all the factors affecting our judgment. It also requires that we listen reflectively and with an open mind to the perspectives of others.

The same thing applies to thinking innovatively. The research is clear that most innovation occurs when diverse teams work together and use innovation ideation and experimentation processes. Diversity brings different perspectives to the table that make it more likely that someone can more easily see what you can't see. To be good at doing what smart machines can't do well, then, requires us to admit that we need to work and collaborate with others and that we need to be the type of person whom others want to work and collaborate with. That means we must be good listeners, trustworthy, and socially sensitive. In the SMA, it doesn't matter whether you're a freelancer, entrepreneur, employee, manager, or leader, you'll need to engage with others in what we call "making meaning together" collaboration, which is very different than normal meeting talk.

### Our fight-flee-or-freeze tendencies

Another way in which our evolutionary nature affects our ability to master SMA Skills is that we are also prehistoric when it comes to responding to stress and anxiety in ways that inhibit our ability to learn, create, or innovate for fear of failure. Our minds haven't caught up to modern life and still respond to any stress as if it threatens our very survival—triggering the older emotional center of our brains (the amygdala) to send out a cascade of hormones and physiological responses that bypass the later-evolved part of the brain where reasoning occurs (the prefrontal cortex) and causing an almost instantaneous fight-flee-or-freeze response. Such a response made sense when saber-toothed tigers were on the loose, but not so much when modern professional demands require that we slow down and think critically and creatively in response to the pressures of the global economy. In today's world, humans cannot fight, flee, or freeze in response to the necessary risks and failures involved in iterative learning.

We're not the first ones to evangelize about how learning, skill development, innovation, and creativity come directly from mistakes and failures. Everyone from Thomas Edison and his ten thousand failed inventions before the light bulb to Michael Jordan and his nine thousand missed shots has made this point. The philosopher Daniel Dennett describes the importance of mistakes in *Intuition Pumps and Other Tools for Thinking*: "Mistakes are not just opportunities for learning; they are, in an important sense, the *only* opportunity for learning or making something truly new."[26]

Having the courage to try, experiment, and learn from the inevitable failures can make sense to most of us logically, but remember we're only human beings, not smart machines (or Michael Jordan, for that matter), and thus we rarely think and behave logically or in our best interests even when we think we are. Our subconscious emotions and behaviors influence our willingness and ability to fail in the process of creating or innovating. It's not just the failure itself—most of us don't even like dealing with the mere uncertainty involved in experimenting. Research has shown that we generally prefer certainty to uncertainty. One study found that we would all rather *definitely* get an electric shock now than *maybe* get shocked later, and we show greater nervous-system activation when we're waiting for an unpredictable shock than an expected one.[27] Our fear of uncertainty is increasingly a problem, because in the SMA, the advance of technology is increasing uncertainty as well as the need to adapt and experiment to stay afloat at work and in daily life.

## We are inwardly focused

A profound problem for us in executing uniquely human SMA Skills is that we usually perceive and process the outside world in an inwardly focused, self-protective manner. This is a result of both nature and nurture. In general, **we're cognitively blind, confirmation-seeking, and emotionally defensive and** reflexive thinkers. We operate more like a defensive closed system than a system open to disconfirming information, differing opinions, or new information that may challenge our stories about who we are and how the world works or to experimenting and opening ourselves up to learning from mistakes and failures.

Staying relevant and optimizing our thinking, listening, relating, and working with others in order to excel at the four SMA Skills will require us to become more of an open system—more open to what's going on in the world outside our heads and more open to others. Our inward focus will need to change to an outward focus with respect to others because it'll be very hard for most all of us to excel at the SMA Skills by ourselves. We'll need the help of others, and that requires that we emotionally relate and connect to them.

Connecting to and relating with other human beings is fundamental to human motivation. That's not anecdote; science has proved it over and over. This need to belong with and attach to others is something innate across cultures, ethnicities, and gender.[28] Many studies have shown that connecting emotionally and building relationships are not just about finding love and friendship and being happy in our personal lives; they're embedded within our drive to live, learn, and succeed. Research shows that students who emotionally connect with a teacher do better in school; employees who emotionally connect with coworkers are more productive; and emotional connection improves client and customer service. We know this intuitively without the data, yet we don't seem to understand or acknowledge the fact that our tendencies to be self-obsessed and our individualistic, hypercompetitive culture are often at odds with making these emotional connections and building these meaningful relationships at work.

That's a real problem in the SMA because higher-level thinking requires us to connect with other people who can help us get past our biases. It's also crucial to engaging in the kind of teamwork and collaboration that leads to creativity and innovation. Most important, as of yet, smart machines, robots, and AI cannot fully replace the kind of empathetic emotional and social connections that humans have with other humans. Geoff Colvin, the author of *Humans Are Underrated,*[29] has gone so far as to suggest that soon jobs requiring deep human interaction may be the only ones left for the masses. In any case, being able to hone our emotional and social skills remains one of our few advantages. The bottom line is that in the SMA very few of us will succeed on our own. We'll need the help of others, which means we'll need to be the kind of people whom others will want to help. That requires much more than being "nice": it means being a trustworthy helper in return.

### Our idea of "smart" no longer works

Another problem for us in developing SMA Skills is that today the dominant definition of "smart" is still quantity based. Today, we think, I'm smarter than you if I know more than you, and the way to determine that is by seeing who makes the fewest mistakes on "tests" of our knowledge and experience. That definition is a legacy of the Industrial Revolution's need for the mass education of workers who could do routine and repetitive manual and cognitive tasks error-free. It's also the consequence of a knowledge-based meritocratic economy, which rewards those who "know" more and "tell" more than those who listen and inquire.

Many of us who are college graduates or knowledge workers have probably defined ourselves in large part by being smarter in this way than others. We succeeded because we knew more, and we measured being smart by the grades and extrinsic rewards we received. Higher grades resulted from accuracy and efficiency—knowing facts fast and making few mistakes or at least knowing facts faster and making fewer mistakes than others. Most of our teachers, coaches, and parents instilled that mindset in us, and, later, managers and employers reinforced it. From our childhoods on we learned the importance of knowing more and making fewer mistakes, and we were led to believe that "smarter" people would get good jobs and succeed.

Another problem with the belief in a quantity-based definition of smart is that it encourages a constant need to prove ourselves by "looking" smart. That in turn motivates people to avoid experimenting and risking mistakes, which inhibits learning, improvement, discovery, innovation, and creativity. That's a huge roadblock because innovation, creativity, and entrepreneurship usually result from iterative learning, when things do not turn out as expected, that is, from surprises or failures.

A quantity-based definition of smart also incites ego protection and reinforces an individualistic culture in which our ultimate goal, even if subconscious, is to view every interaction as a way to compare ourselves or compete with others—a way to prove our intelligence or "win" the conversation or transaction. That kind of self-focus leads to ego defensiveness and fear that inhibits learning and impedes critical thinking, creativity, innovation, and emotional engagement with others. In sum, in the SMA our old quantity-based notion of smart, what we call Old Smart, is the new "stupid." Knowledge workers, you've been warned.

## We Need New Mindsets and New Behaviors

Cultivating SMA Skills in today's and future workforces goes far beyond institutional training or challenges—it goes to the very heart of our human nature, our social and organizational cultures, and our daily behaviors. We believe that to truly excel at the higher-level thinking and emotional engagement underlying the SMA Skills requires us to engage in four key behaviors: **Quieting Ego; Managing Self** (one's thinking and emotions); **Reflective Listening;** and **Otherness** (emotionally connecting and relating to others).

As we explain in more detail in Part 2, we determined these to be the most fundamental common behaviors underlying SMA Skills, based on researching hundreds of academic articles and over forty-five leading books about those four SMA Skills. Unfortunately, most of us don't regularly engage in those behaviors. In many ways they're in fact counterintuitive to us. To thrive and lead others in the SMA, then, requires many of us to work hard at behavioral improvements, and that's much easier if the new behaviors fit well with our mental models.

Mental models guide our thoughts and actions and predispose us to behave in certain ways. They can help us simplify the world and operate efficiently, but they can also be limiting and destructive when they're like concrete bunkers, blinding or repelling us from ideas, facts, or perspectives that challenge our views of the world. Many of our mental models are stuck in ideas and perceptions originating in the Industrial Revolution. The SMA is a new reality requiring new ideas and rules.

For most of us, our mental model is dominated by a quantitative definition of smart and an obsessively self-absorbed and individualistic, winner-take-all approach to life and livelihood that inhibits the more outwardly focused behaviors necessary to excel at SMA Skills. Developing the behaviors and ultimately the skills that will give us a chance for human excellence in the SMA, then, requires that we first change our mental model of what it means to be smart and what it takes to succeed.

---

### Reflection Time

Periodically throughout the book we pause and invite you to reflect and "make meaning" of what you have read. What we're asking you to do is "try on" the ideas, consider how it would feel if you believed those ideas, or think deeply about how the specific points affect you. We suggest that you write down your answers and use them as a reflective journal to come back to on your journey to human excellence.

1. Think about your job. How much of what you do is the same every day? How much of what you do can be broken down into small repeatable steps? What does that mean?

2. How much of what you do requires rigorous, deliberate, and focused critical or innovative thinking?

3. How much of what you do requires high-level emotional engagement with other people?

4. Do you accept the science of how we're often cognitively and emotionally reflexive in our thinking? If not, why not? What is the basis of your belief? What scientific research are you relying on?

5. How do you define "smart"?

---

# 2

# NewSmart: A New Definition of "Smart"

Updating our mental model for the SMA is analogous to updating a computer's operating system. Most of us have been taught to define what it means to be smart and what it takes to succeed based on Industrial Revolution–era thinking that doesn't account for the latest science of higher-level human thinking and relating. We're in a new era in which technology will, in many more cases, be smarter than us, and that will affect whether we'll work, how we'll work, and what we'll do at work. Our outdated mentality will stifle our abilities to learn and adapt in the midst of rapid technological advancement, the dynamic global economy, and ever-increasing competition for the decreasing number of jobs available for humans.

Here's a personal example of the power of mental models. I (Ed) was on a trip to London to give a keynote talk about the concepts in this book. My wife and I visited the British Museum of Natural History and were having our lunch break in the museum's dining room. My wife had ordered a side of French fries. While we were drinking our tea and waiting for our lunch, the waiter brought my wife a very small plate that was half-filled with ketchup for the fries. I was aghast. They filled only half of that tiny plate with ketchup? What cheap-skates! I was miffed and considered confronting the waiter, but decided that if my wife wanted more ketchup she could ask for it. Then our lunch arrived, and after I accepted my wife's offer of a fry, she asked: "With ketchup or mayonnaise?"

Sure enough, the ketchup plate was filled with mayonnaise on the other half, and I didn't see it. My brain didn't process the stimuli because my mental model was that people ate fries with ketchup, not mayonnaise. I was cognitively blind, and that was scary. I had actually stared at that plate in emotional outrage and physically did not see the mayonnaise in front of my face.

Our mental models affect how we perceive the world and in some cases can actually distort or misrepresent reality. Our models may also greatly differ from other people's models and thus their views of reality. Jack Mezirow, an adult learning expert, explains that "we have a strong tendency to reject ideas that fail to fit our preconception,"[1] but he also explains that we can "transform our frames of reference [mental models] through critical reflection on the assumptions upon which our interpretations, beliefs, and habits of mind or points of view are based."[2]

To change our mental model for the SMA, we first need to accept a quality-based definition of "being smart"— a NewSmart—that we define as excelling at the highest level of thinking, learning, and emotionally engaging with others that one is capable of doing. NewSmart is a measure not of *what* you know or *how much* you know but of

- the quality of your thinking, listening, collaborating, and learning;

- how good you are at "not" knowing and decoupling your beliefs (not values) from your ego;
- how good you are at being open to continually stress-testing your beliefs about how the world works; and
- how good you are at trying out new ideas and ways to accomplish your objectives and learning from those experiments.

## The Genesis of NewSmart

During Ed's early consulting on the topics of this book with business executives and leaders, he realized that many of them had a hard time accepting the science that we discussed in chapter 1, which clearly demonstrates that most of us are suboptimal thinkers and that our egos and fears get in the way of learning. He often used the term *learners anonymous* and invited participants to say out loud, "I am a suboptimal thinker, listener, relator, and collaborator." Few people wanted to or could do it. After all, many of these folks considered themselves already very "smart" and successful. One senior leader told Ed, "My mind worked well enough to get me here!"

What many of those skeptical executives and leaders did accept, however, was the increasing evidence that technology will transform the workplace by assuming all the activities that technology can do as well as or better than humans and that smart machines will know and process more data faster and more accurately than humans. They also acknowledged the expert opinions that humans will be left to perform higher-level thinking skills, to emotionally engage with other humans, and to continually experiment, learn, and adapt to rapid change characterized by high uncertainty. In other words, they were able to understand that humans can't compete on "smarts," at least not in the traditional way we have come to understand that term. It was a story that made sense to most of them.

Coming to terms with NewSmart was also a personal process for us. We also needed to make sense of the science of learning and the impact that recent and relentless technological advancement will have on our careers. We, too, needed to embrace a new definition of smart, because we also were heavily invested in Old Smart behaviors and came to understand how they inhibited us.

So what does the high-quality thinking, learning, and emotional engagement underlying NewSmart look like in practice? We've determined that the following five principles exemplify NewSmart:

1. I'm defined not by what I know or how much I know, but by the quality of my thinking, listening, relating, and collaborating.
2. My mental models are not reality—they are only my generalized stories of how my world works.
3. I'm not my ideas, and I must decouple my beliefs (not values) from my ego.
4. I must be open-minded and treat my beliefs (not values) as hypotheses to be constantly tested and subject to modification by better data.
5. My mistakes and failures are opportunities to learn.

Those particular ideas emerged from our study of the following sources: Greek philosophy, the scientific method, psychological science (cognitive, social, developmental, experimental, educational, clinical, and positive), behavioral economics, critical and innovative thinking experts, and several market-leading businesses, including Pixar Animation Studios and Bridgewater Associates. We'll discuss the meaning behind each principle in turn.

**1. I'm defined not by what I know or how much I know but by the quality of my thinking, listening, relating, and collaborating.**

This bedrock NewSmart principle is based on the following critical thinking mantra created by Richard Paul and Linda Elder in *Critical Thinking: Tools for Taking Charge of Your Professional and Personal Life*: "I will not identify with the content of any belief. I will only identify with the way I come to my beliefs."

For me (Ed), those statements were startling. Why? Because my ego was heavily invested in knowing more than other people, going all the way back to my elementary school days. I had defined myself as very "smart" and took great pride in being smarter than most people—at least in my eyes. I strived to be the fastest smart person in the room and verbalize any answer before anyone else could beat me to the punch. I was that kid in the second grade sitting in the front row always waving his hand wildly until the teacher called on him.

I formed my definition of success early in my life in part because of my circumstances. I grew up in rural Georgia, where boys are taught to be strong and powerful and typically demonstrate those attributes by playing football. I was not that. I was too slow and weak, and I was the only boy in my grade not chosen to play in the peewee football league. No kidding—the *only* boy. It was humiliating and made me feel like an outsider (it's still a little embarrassing to write about).

Because I wasn't going to make my parents proud of me or feel good about myself through athletics, I had to find another way.

Thankfully, I was blessed with a computational mind and could memorize a lot of facts and do arithmetic in my head accurately and quickly. So I started competing at being "smart," and that meant striving to have the right answer every day in every class and having it faster than anyone else. I competed on tests. I competed in weekly spelling and Bible bees. I competed in weekly memorization tests. At age seven, I had discovered a principle of competing that worked pretty well for me professionally for decades.

I eventually learned not to wave my hand so wildly, but I always placed a premium on beating others—speaking first whenever there was an opportunity or interrupting anyone who wasn't my boss to get the answer in before anyone else. My ego, in other words, was heavily invested in Old Smart. My self-worth was tied up in my answers. My identity depended on the speed and correctness of those answers. I *was* my answers, and that meant that I had to strongly defend my position and attack everyone else's. I was a know-it-all, although I did try to be a nice one—to be agreeable and mild-mannered—so I thought it was all OK. Instead, I was doing what Paul and Elder stated a good critical thinker should not do—identifying with the content of my beliefs.

Recognizing that was a wow moment, but I also quickly understood that it could be liberating. If I could decouple my ego from my beliefs—if I could stop worrying about knowing more or looking smart, then I could be more open-minded and less emotionally defensive (which has also been a big problem for me). With that first sentence—**I will not identify with**

the content of any belief—I could replace Old Smart by defining myself in accordance with the second sentence: the way I
come to my beliefs. Those two statements were transformational, and as I look back on it now, I realize that they started
me on the most gratifying learning journey of my life.

### How do you define yourself?

Assume for a minute that, like Ed, you identify with your
answers—that having your answer or position validated and
looking smart is important to your ego and feeling good about
yourself. That means that you don't want to look "not smart,"
which you believe happens when you're wrong or make
mistakes. It also means that you want to be right, and being
right means other people have to be wrong. Can you see how
that mental model makes the open-mindedness required for
higher-level thinking nearly impossible, and collaboration
becomes a competition to see *who* is right rather than *what* is
right? Can you see that being heavily invested in being all-knowing and "right" can limit your ability to listen to and consider
differing views? And can you see how it makes you defensive
if someone questions you or challenges your thinking?

How we define ourselves drives our behaviors and our
interpretations of the world. Many of us are invested in being
right, not making mistakes, not looking bad, and being liked
or admired by others. We try to behave in ways that affirm
our view of ourselves, and we try to avoid behaving in ways
that would diminish our view of ourselves. In this way, we're
a "closed system," always inwardly focused on protecting and
defending ourselves.

That kind of inward focus can lead to closed-mindedness
and ineffective thinking and learning relationships. It can also

result in being self-absorbed, self-protective, and preoccupied with feeling special and better than others—that is, a "big me" mentality that inhibits our ability to build relationships and collaborate with others, which is necessary for thriving in the SMA.

---

**Reflection Time**

How do *you* think?

How do you know when to think deliberately?

What do you *do* when you think?

---

*How do you come to your beliefs?*

Now that we've thought about why we shouldn't define ourselves by what or how much we know, let's think about what we should define ourselves by—the quality our thinking, listening, relating, and collaborating. Let's do that by probing the second sentence of Paul and Elder's critical thinking mantra: "I will identify only with the way I come to my beliefs."

Take a moment to think about that.

How do you come to your beliefs or answers?

I (Ed) realized that I hadn't spent much time thinking deeply about *how* my beliefs were formed or how I think. I hadn't been trained to think critically. My early professional training in law and later in finance was to think analytically, solve puzzles, and manipulate numbers quickly in my head—all the stuff smart machines can now do. I'd already learned quite a bit about how innovators think and the processes innovators used, and I had studied creative thinkers and knew the differences between convergent and divergent thinking. I also knew of cognitive biases and cognitive dissonance, but I didn't self-manage my thinking and I didn't use processes to check my thinking. I have since learned in my work that I'm not alone in having not thought deeply about *how* I think.

Over the past few years I've asked all my consulting clients—hundreds of very successful senior business managers and leaders—"*How* do you think?" Common answers are "it just happens" or "stuff just pops up in my mind" or "it comes naturally."

Considering these questions initially led me (Ed) to take a look at Daniel Kahneman's research. His 2011 book *Thinking, Fast and Slow* was a deep dive into critical thinking. It was a hard read and showed me that I needed to study critical thinking in depth. After reading lots of other books and academic research, I created a personal Critical Thinking Purposes Checklist and a list of Critical Thinking Questions to help me be a better thinker. We provide a copy of those tools in chapter 5.

Defining ourselves by the quality of our thinking doesn't just mean adopting different processes or routines, however. It means acknowledging that we can't do it alone, because the science is clear on that. To do our best critical and innovative thinking, we need the help of others. We need to think out loud with other people and listen to their feedback, critiques, and differing perspectives, and that happens best when we think with people who have had a variety of training and experiences.

In turn, it's easier for other people to help us if we view collaboration not as a competition to see who is right but rather as a conversation to find the most accurate answer. In the SMA, we must recognize that we're competing not with others (Old Smart) but against the limitations of our own minds (NewSmart).

| Old Smart | NewSmart |
|-----------|----------|
| I know | I'm good at not knowing |
| I tell | I ask |

---

**Reflection Time**

How do you define yourself?

What is your ego heavily invested in?

Are you focused on *looking good* at what you do or on *improving* what you do?

Are you concerned with *who* is right or *what* is right?

In what circumstances are you prone to being emotionally defensive?

What does that tell you? How would it feel to define yourself by the quality of your thinking, listening, relating, and collaborating?

---

**2. My mental models are not reality—they are only my generalized stories of how my world works.**

**3. I'm not my ideas, and I must decouple my beliefs (not values) from my ego.**

We discussed Paul and Elder's admonition to not identify with the content of our beliefs, and we have learned from science that our mental models are only our subjective, internal story of how the world works. We were pleased to discover that Ed Catmull, cofounder of Pixar, brought business validation to those views. Pixar is a computer animation film studio that is now a division of Disney. It has produced ten Academy Award–nominated and eight Academy Award–winning films, including *Finding Nemo, The Incredibles, Ratatouille, WALL-E, Up, Toy Story 3, Brave,* and *Inside Out.* Catmull's book *Creativity, Inc.,* which he co-authored with Amy Wallace, is the story of how he and his team created a high-performance creative company. Catmull explains how to create the kind of work environment that mitigates the two big inhibitors of learning and creativity: ego and fear. He describes how Pixar works to mitigate those inhibitors through its culture and management processes, so that its people will seek out and use daily feedback from colleagues.

Catmull explains the company's position on ego: "You are not your idea, and if you identify too closely with your ideas, you will take offense when they are challenged."[3] He also describes its position on mental models: "Our mental models aren't reality. They are tools, like the models weather forecasters use to predict the weather. But, as we know all too well, sometimes the forecast says rain and, boom, the sun comes out. The tool is not reality."[4] As Catmull describes it, Pixar in effect operationalized Paul and Elder's statement: "I will not identify with the content of any belief."

Over the last two years of consulting, I (Ed) have found that the phrases "I am not my ideas" and "my mental models are not reality" really stick with people and help them make sense of the NewSmart standard. By providing a reason to become less heavily invested in one's ideas or one's interpretations of how the world works, these two concepts related to high-quality thinking and learning also reinforce the ones we discuss next. They make it easier to be open-minded, to treat your beliefs (we're not talking about values) as hypotheses to be tested, and to treat *idea* failures not as *personal* failures but as learning opportunities.

| Old Smart | NewSmart |
|---|---|
| Defend my views | Improve my views |
| Seek confirmation | Seek truth |

### 4. I must be open-minded and treat my beliefs (not values) as hypotheses to be constantly tested and subject to modification by better data.

This NewSmart idea comes from the scientific method and was made even more powerful through Ed's research of the high-performance learning system at Bridgewater Associates. Have you ever heard of the phrase "being good at not knowing"? Like us, you've probably spent most of your career being paid to "know." But being comfortable with and managing ignorance—*not* knowing—is key to how scientists think and is fundamental to the scientific method.

"Being good at not knowing" is one of the fundamentals of Ray Dalio, who founded Bridgewater Associates. Dalio has published his full set of over two hundred *Principles* of life and management on Bridgewater's website.[5] Reading Dalio's *Principles* in 2011 started Ed on a three-year study of Bridgewater that culminated in featuring the company's culture and management practices in his last book, *Learn or Die: Using Science to Build a Leading-Edge Learning Organization*,[6] which focused on using the science of learning as the basis for creating a high-performance learning organization. Ed found that more than any leader he'd come across in fourteen years of researching the DNA of high-performing organizations, Dalio had confronted head on the two big learning and thinking inhibitors—ego and fear—through his *Principles*, company culture, and daily learning processes.

Dalio states in *Principles* that "being wary about overconfidence and good at not knowing" are crucial in the search for truth. Dalio has said that he needs "independent thinkers," innovative thinkers not imprisoned by their mental models, in order to excel in his business.[7] He believes that independent thinkers are people who strive to figure out what they believe and why they believe it and to have their beliefs tested by others.[8]

Dalio was important in our study of NewSmart because he designed his *Principles*, which became his organizational culture, to enable and promote behaviors that lead to independent thinking unrestrained by ego defensiveness or fears of being wrong and looking stupid. Dalio had been at this for decades, and it was comforting to learn that it took the best and brightest people he hired about eighteen months of daily work with real-time feedback to overcome their reflexive and defensive ways of thinking and move toward becoming high-quality thinkers. Those data confirmed that the journey, though incredibly difficult, was achievable by focusing on improving a few behaviors at a time through the daily use of processes and by regularly measuring progress.

### Embracing ignorance

The concept of not knowing is humbling and uncomfortable, but it's a concept we can trace back thousands of years to Socrates, who said, "I know nothing except the fact of my ignorance," and to Confucius, who is reputed to have said, "Real knowledge is knowing the extent of one's ignorance." All of this goes to the heart of intellectual humility and scientific thinking. In *Ignorance: How It Drives Science*, Stuart Firestein, professor and chair of Columbia University's Department of Biological Sciences, explains: "Scientists don't concentrate on what they know, which is considerable but also miniscule, but rather on what they don't know."[9]

In contrast, Kahneman describes the opposite of being good at "not knowing" and our proclivity to make broad generalizations based on little data in *Thinking, Fast and Slow* as "the puzzling limitation of our mind" to have "excessive confidence in what we believe we know, and our apparent inability to acknowledge the full extent of our ignorance and the uncertainty of the world we live in."[10]

Ed was reminded of this common human fallacy within a couple of weeks of writing this chapter by his scientist-trained wife, when during a discussion she told him, "You are making a big generalization based on two data points." She was correct.

Those of us not in the hard sciences—for example, physics, biology, and chemistry—have not been trained in a detailed, methodical process of "if this, then that." Most of us nonscientists consider "if this, then *maybe* that," because *this* and *that* seem to occur together frequently. Understanding the difference is the first step in being good at not knowing, accepting the magnitude of our ignorance, and thinking more like a scientist, which we believe is crucial for the higher-level thinking required to excel at SMA Skills.

Good scientists are open-minded, and they treat their beliefs as hypotheses to constantly test and subject to modification by better data. Scientific thinking is not simply a matter of designing experiments to isolate variables to determine whether cause–effect relationships exist, however. Good scientists also have to approach the process with a truly open mind—something much easier said than done and something almost all of us struggle to do. The kind of inquiry-based process at the heart of scientific thinking must go hand in hand with open-mindedness, because without open-mindedness the hypothesis testing at the root of scientific method is compromised.

Experts always identify open-mindedness as a key aspect of critical thinking, creativity, and innovation. In *Handbook on Character Strengths and Virtues*, the psychologists Christopher Peterson and Martin Seligman provide the consensus definition of open-mindedness as the "willingness to search actively for evidence against one's favored beliefs, plans, or goals, and to weigh such evidence fairly when it's available."[11]

Mark Pagel, a professor of evolutionary biology at the University of Reading, advocates that we treat *all* knowledge as a hypothesis: "The elusive nature of knowledge should remind us to be humble when interpreting it and acting on it, and this should grant us both a tolerance and skepticism toward others and their interpretations. Knowledge should always be treated as a hypothesis."[12]

Max Tegmark, an MIT physics professor, says the following about a scientific approach: "The core of a scientific lifestyle is to change your mind when faced with information that disagrees with your views, avoiding intellectual inertia."[13] Italian theoretical physicist Carlo Rovelli states it this way: "A good scientist will be ready to shift to a different point of view if better evidence or novel arguments emerge."[14] In *Critical Think-*

*ing,* Paul and Elder likewise made the point that good thinkers are ready to drop or change any belief that cannot be credibly supported by evidence and are ready to follow evidence wherever it takes them.[15]

---

### Reflection Time

Do you, as a matter of course, ask yourself, "Why do I believe this?"

Do you, as a matter of course, unpack the assumptions you're making that underlie your conclusion?

Do you ask yourself whether you have enough credible data to believe that so strongly?

Do you, as a matter of course, actively search for evidence of being wrong?

---

### Thinking like a scientist

What does it mean to think like a scientist in practice and embrace those principles in real life? It means acknowledging that our biases, ego, and emotional defensiveness could be getting in the way. It means we should be open-minded and seek out conflicting data by testing our beliefs with other knowledgeable people and asking them, "Do you agree or disagree?" and "What am I missing?"

Can you see how adopting a mental model that our beliefs are conditional and subject to modification by new or better data is liberating? Instead of feeling that we have to immediately and reactively defend our views, it allows us to be open-minded and really explore other views, all in search of the truth. That in turn reinforces the NewSmart idea to define ourselves not by *what* we believe but by *how we think.* Being good at not knowing and accepting the magnitude of our ignorance should help us be wary of overconfidence and reduce our defensiveness when others disagree with us or challenge the factual foundation or logical basis of our reasoning. Thinking like a scientist and treating our beliefs as hypotheses subject to modification by data likewise should make it easier for us not to identify so strongly with our beliefs and to be less defensive. It all fits together in a self-reinforcing way.

| Old Smart | NewSmart |
| --- | --- |
| Closed mind | Open mind |
| Insecure if beliefs are challenged | Insecure if beliefs are NOT challenged |

In talking with employees at Bridgewater Associates, Ed remembers one of them making a statement like this: "Instead of feeling insecure when my thinking is challenged, I now feel insecure if my thinking is not challenged."

## 5. My mistakes and failures are opportunities to learn.

Innovation, creativity, entrepreneurship, and most learning results from an iterative, trial-and-error process of trying new things, experimenting, and building prototypes that will in most cases fail to achieve the desired results. You can't avoid mistakes if you want to be an innovator, creator, or entrepreneur. Innovative companies have told us that their failure rates on small experiments can be as high as 90 percent. As Steven Johnson explains in *Where Good Ideas Come From: The Natural History of Innovation*, "The history of being spectacularly right has a shadow history lurking behind it: a much longer history of being spectacularly wrong, again and again. And not just wrong, but messy."[16]

In fact, the more willing you are to experiment and learn from mistakes, the faster you'll reach a viable solution. In the SMA, this will be a highly valued skill, because it's likely that operational excellence (better, faster, and cheaper) will become technology-driven and commoditized in many industries, leaving creativity and innovation as the key value-creation processes. The Old Smart belief that mistakes are bad will not work in a fast-changing, technology-driven world in which innovation and creativity will most likely be the real value generators for most businesses.

The key is to learn from each mistake and not make the same one again, to not make "bet the ranch" type of mistakes, and to get help from others to test your thinking before taking important actions. Dalio's *Principles* also emphasize that mistakes should be viewed as learning opportunities. This sentiment is common in Silicon Valley entrepreneurial folklore as well as among the famous stories about the failures of successful inventors like Thomas Edison. Unfortunately, despite the presence of these stories in popular culture, all mistakes are bad from the viewpoint of Old Smart. And, thus, many of us fear making mistakes.

### Fear of mistakes

Fear is a negative emotion, and we've already explained how negative emotions narrow our thinking and can lead to poor judgments. In studying Intuit for his last book, Ed discovered that the company has a pervasive learn-by-experimentation culture and goes so far as to avoid using the term *mistakes* to mitigate the fear of making them. Intuit has a culture of referring to the unexpected results of experimentation as "surprises."

As the world-renowned psychologist Mihaly Csikszentmihalyi states in *Creativity: Flow and the Psychology of Discovery and Invention*, "Each of us is born with two contradictory sets of instructions: a conservative tendency, made up of instincts for self-preservation, self-aggrandizement, and saving energy, and an expansive tendency made up of instincts for exploring, for enjoying novelty and risk—the curiosity that leads to creativity belongs to this set."[17] Unfortunately, many of us cling to the first instinct. Fear of mistakes and failure can also be a self-focused emotion driven by a self-focused need to be perfect.

### The perfectionism problem

Researcher Brené Brown has found that what often holds people back from new challenges, experimenting, or facing uncertainty is a preoccupation with perfectionism and the shame that arises when we aren't perfect. As Brown explains, "Research shows that perfectionism hampers achievement. Perfectionism is correlated with depression, anxiety, addiction, and life paralysis or missed opportunities. The fear of failing, making mistakes, not meeting people's expectations, and being criticized keeps us outside of the arena where healthy competition and striving unfolds."[18]

Brown's description of the culture and mental models that fuel perfectionism and shame sound a lot like Old Smart and the kind of self-absorption that is the opposite of Humility:

Perfectionism is, at its core, about trying to earn approval. Most perfectionists grew up being praised for achievement and performance (grades, manners, rule following, people

53

pleasing, appearance, sports). Somewhere along the way, they adopted this dangerous and debilitating belief system: "I am what I accomplish and how well I accomplish it. Please. Perform. Perfect."[19]

I (Katherine) have struggled with this inhibiting belief system my whole life. Sure, it was a source of debilitating stress and anxiety at times, but I had always considered my type A perfectionism as the basis of my success in school and at work (no pain, no gain, right?). That is, until I read Carol Dweck's book *Mindset*. Her research made me realize that perfectionism is just another way of wanting and having your ego tied up in looking "smart"—in valuing "performing" over "learning." Dweck, a psychologist, conducted decades of groundbreaking research on motivation and found that people who had *learning goals*—in which one pursues mastery and growth—greatly differed in terms of the type and the endurance of their motivation as well as actual achievement outcomes from people who had *performance goals*—in which one's goal is to impress others, look smart, or receive extrinsic rewards—that is, the good grade, the award, the praise.

Dweck and other researchers found that learning goals lead to greater and more enduring intrinsic motivation as well as greater actual achievement. She also found that learning goals are associated with a *growth mindset*, in which one believes implicitly that intelligence and abilities are the results of effort and perseverance, while performance goals are associated with a *fixed mindset*, in which one believes implicitly that intelligence and talent are innate and largely unchangeable.

According to Dweck, many people's personal mindsets are influenced by how their parents and teachers praised them.

When parents praise children for their intelligence and their talent—for example, "You're so smart!"—Dweck says that it gives kids a boost, but only for a moment: "The minute they hit a snag, their confidence goes out the window and their motivation hits rock bottom. If success means they're smart, then failure means they're dumb. That's the fixed mindset."[20]

If Ed was that kid in the first row waving his hand wildly, then I was the kind of fixed-mindset kid Dweck described above—refraining from raising my hand for fear of not being perfect. Personally, I don't blame my parents for this. I think my personality and temperament were predisposed to a fixed mindset, which I suspect was implicitly reinforced by the broader culture of Old Smart. From a young age, I withdrew from anything at which I couldn't almost immediately excel to avoid shame and not being seen as smart or talented—or I simply blamed other people for my failures. Strike out at softball? Time to quit. Miss a few questions on a test? Ego is crushed until I decide the test must have had a design flaw. Unable to outargue my assertive criminal law classmates? Corporate law is suddenly much more interesting. What many viewed as a lack of self-confidence—something women are often associated with—was actually hyper self-focus and a desire to protect my image.

### The right kinds of mistakes

Accepting mistakes as learning opportunities can help you get out of this cycle of perfectionism and failure avoidance that limits motivation, learning, creativity, and innovation and can help you view mistakes in a less personal and emotionally defensive way. A couple of caveats here: we're not at all suggesting that every mistake and failure is acceptable, particularly if you're making the same mistakes over and over. That's not learning.

In *Creative Confidence: Unleashing the Creative Potential within Us All*, IDEO founders Tom Kelley and David Kelley explain that to learn from failure, you have to "own" it and "figure out what went wrong and what to do better next time."[21] Neither are we suggesting that you take more risks or start making more mistakes if they will negatively affect your job and career. We accept the fact that many organizations support an Old Smart mentality and will be slow to tolerate more failure in the name of learning. If you're working on or leading a team involved in problem solving, innovation, or doing something very new for the business, engage others in a discussion about mistakes and what types of mistakes are good learning opportunities. See if you can create an approach that works in your unit.

| Old Smart | NewSmart |
|---|---|
| Mistakes are bad | Mistakes are learning opportunities |
| Perfectionism | Learning |

Collectively, the ideas that underlie the quality-based standard of NewSmart codify the best of what science, real-world examples, and experience have taught us about how to think and continually learn and to embrace more outwardly focused behaviors required in order to excel at the four SMA Skills. NewSmart is already relevant today, but its importance will rise to mission critical over the next decade, as the SMA engulfs many workplaces. Whether you work for a big company or a small company or you're a freelancer or entrepreneur, your success will depend on the quality of your thinking and your abilities to connect and emotionally engage with other people.

In the next chapter we probe further into the second hero of our SMA Story: Humility. We'll explain why we believe that embracing a mindset of Humility lays the groundwork for meeting NewSmart ideals and is, thus, the gateway to human excellence in the SMA.

---

### Reflection Time

Please read each NewSmart idea and carefully ask yourself these questions:

    What does this mean to me?

    Does this make sense to me?

    How would this help me?

    How could it hurt me?

    Will I adopt this idea?

    Why or why not?

1. I'm defined not by what I know or how much I know but by the quality of my thinking, listening, relating, and collaborating.
2. My mental models are not reality—they are only my generalized stories of how my world works.
3. I'm not my ideas, and I must decouple my beliefs (not values) from my ego.
4. I must be open-minded and treat my beliefs (not values) as hypotheses to be constantly tested and subject to modification by better data.
5. My mistakes and failures are opportunities to learn.

---

# 3

# Humility: The Gateway to Human Excellence in the SMA

When you think of humility, what immediately comes to mind? Mother Teresa serving the poor and sick? Jesus washing the feet of his disciples? The Dalai Lama meditating in his monk robes? That's pretty typical. Certainly, humility as a concept has strong religious resonance. When we think of humility, most of us consider people who are very spiritual or devout or who have altruistically dedicated their entire lives to serving others. Most of us don't immediately think of hedge fund managers or the heads of global corporations.

Humility is rarely associated with intellectual aptitude or professional success in Western societies, especially in the United States. That's because synonyms for *humility* in common Western parlance often include *lowliness*, *meekness*, and *submissiveness*—characteristics that would seem to be the antithesis of achievement and success. Our definition of Humility and our belief in its power as a mindset, however, comes not from these lowly connotations but from our study of it as a philosophical intellectual virtue and psychological construct: We define **Humility as a mindset about oneself that is open-minded, self-accurate, and "not all about me,"** and that enables one to embrace the world as it "is" in the pursuit of human excellence.

That doesn't mean thinking less *of yourself*, but it does mean thinking *about yourself* less (e.g., how you look; what other people are thinking or saying about you; how you're coming across; how you're being judged). The Foundation for Critical Thinking views this kind of mindset as an intellectual strength and a cornerstone of critical thinking. It explains that "intellectual humility does not imply spinelessness or submissiveness. It implies the lack of intellectual pretentiousness, boastfulness, or conceit, combined with insight into the logical foundations, or lack of such foundations, of one's beliefs."[1]

What ultimately is needed to thrive in the coming SMA is this kind of openness to perceiving and processing the world more as it *is* and not merely as we believe or would like it to be. That is what's at the heart of our definition of Humility. In the SMA, we all will have to acknowledge the need to spend less time focused on "big me" and instead balance our competitive spirit with a collaborative spirit, because critical thinking, innovative thinking, and high emotional engagement are all team sports—"big us."

## Misperceptions of Humility

We know what you're probably thinking at this point—that everything you've experienced in your life so far indicates that to succeed in our fast-paced, competitive modern world requires a certain level of hyperfocused self-interest, and that to stop believing in your own greatness and instead acknowledge and accept your weaknesses is itself a weakness. Together with other recent phenomena such as the pressure and opportunity for endless self-broadcasting on social media, we have, as many cultural observers have remarked, encouraged a culture of big me and even spawned an alarming increase in clinical narcissism rates.[2]

Even if we don't consider ourselves part of the "big me" cultural phenomenon, for many of us to feel good about ourselves we have to constantly be "right," self-enhance, self-promote, and conceal our weaknesses, all of which drives ego defensiveness and failure intolerance that impede higher-level thinking and relating. Research has shown that self-enhancement bias is in fact quite common. Most people do it reflexively—they take credit for their successes and blame others for their failures. This is called self-serving bias.[3]

Moreover, we have somewhat of a cultural obsession with high self-esteem as the marker of psychological health. The problem, as the psychologist Kristin Neff explains, is that to have high self-esteem, particularly in the United States, we have to feel "special" and "above average" in comparison with others, and that is logically impossible to do all of the time unless we constantly puff ourselves up or put others down. While some psychologists argue that positive illusions can aid psychological well-being in some situations, the problem for higher-level thinking and learning should be obvious—if you tell yourself you're better than you are or you refuse to accept ego-threatening information, you prevent learning and improvement in the areas you need it. That's going to be a major downfall for many in the SMA.

As we describe in chapter 1, the world of work will likely change in fundamental ways, and the march of technology is reaching a point at which none of us can rely on the old rules of success. Cultural and organizational models will of necessity reflect a new reality that is less individually and inwardly focused and more outwardly focused on expanding our think-ing and connecting to others:

| Old Cultural Ways | New Cultural Ways |
|---|---|
| Individuals win | Teams win |
| Play cards close to the chest | Transparency |
| Highest-ranking person can trump | Best idea or argument wins |
| Listening to confirm | Listening to learn |
| Telling | Asking questions |
| Knowing | Being good at not knowing |
| IQ | IQ & EQ |
| Mistakes are always bad | Mistakes are learning opportunities |
| Compete | Collaborate |
| Self-promote | Self-reflect |

Humility may seem somewhat countercultural now, but in the SMA it will be a professional asset. From a global perspec-tive, Humility has long been promoted as a personal and pro-fessional quality in East Asian cultures as well as in Scandinavia through the "law of Jante"—a cultural principle that means no one is to think he or she is better than anyone else and that is said to influence the organizational cultures of such com-panies as Volvo, Ikea, and Ericsson. To truly understand the value of Humility and our definition, you need to understand the philosophy and psychology that informs it.

### The Forgotten Legacy of Intellectual Humility

As a philosophical and theoretical concept, humility has been viewed as the path to learning and enlightenment since ancient times and the intellectual humility of Socrates and Confucius. The Socratic method, which many consider a cornerstone of Western philosophy, is based on the theory that true knowledge results through hypothesis and the right kind of questioning. In ancient Greek society, Socrates publicly questioned his own beliefs and exposed the ignorance of others, particularly the elite of the time, through successively deeper inquiry. He believed that learning occurs only by continually testing our beliefs and answers to essential questions against facts. Socrates surely had intellectual humility, and in many ways he represents the patron saint of critical thinking in Western culture. Anyone who has experienced the Socratic method in a classroom or any context can similarly attest to it being a humbling experience.

Humility was also one of the core values that the Chinese philosopher and politician Confucius espoused in his teachings and writings on education and social interaction. In fact, Confucius is believed to have said that "humility is the solid foundation of all the virtues"—the other Confucian learning virtues being sincerity, diligence, endurance of hardship, perseverance, concentration, and respect for teachers.

Our individualistic Western approach to learning and thinking has in many ways distorted the purpose of Socratic inquiry, using it to justify the hypercriticism and rejection of others' ideas and beliefs and an individual focus on learning and achievement. In studying a Confucian/Socratic framework for analyzing cultural influences on academic learning, the Canadian psychologists Roger Tweed and Darrin Lehman explain that a Socratic learning culture in which questioning the ideas of others is a way to assert one's independence "fulfills the cultural ideal of individualism,"[4] which is so prevalent in the West.

Forgetting the intellectual humility at the heart of Socratic values, we in the West have, in a sense, corrupted and co-opted his essential philosophy of questioning and used it to shout our own beliefs from the rooftops while tearing everyone else's down, all the while viewing it as a high-minded, intellectual affair. We've taken the doubting of everyone else's beliefs and knowledge to heart but seem to have forgotten to turn that lens on ourselves, and we've used this skepticism of others to devalue listening and perspective taking.

## The Psychology of Humility

In psychology, humility has been studied as a personality state and trait, a character strength, an intellectual virtue, a behavior, and a theory of mind. There has been a recent and growing focus on defining, assessing, and measuring a universal concept of humility, as well as a growing body of psychological literature that correlates humility with higher physical and psychological well-being and intrapersonal and interpersonal advantages, particularly in the context of intellectual concerns, metacognitive abilities, leadership, and relationship building.[5]

Carol Dweck and colleagues have found a positive connection between intellectual humility—defined as "acknowledging the partial nature of one's understanding and valuing others' intelligence"—and learning goals (rather than performance goals) as well as actual achievement. In other words, they found that humility boosts learning.

According to the psychologists June Price Tangey, Christopher Peterson, and Martin E. P. Seligman, the psychological attributes of humility are

1. having an accurate (not over- or underestimated) view of one's abilities and achievements;
2. being able to acknowledge one's mistakes, imperfections, gaps in knowledge, and limitations;
3. being open to new ideas, contradictory information, and advice;
4. keeping one's abilities and accomplishments in perspective;
5. having a low focus on self or a tendency to "forget the self"; and
6. appreciating the value of all things and the many different ways other people and things contribute to the world.

Can you see how those attributes would make you more prone to engage in the kinds of behaviors that lead to NewSmart and the higher-level thinking, learning, and emotional engagement required for SMA Skills?

Humility in the context of these psychological tenets is similar to the philosophical principle of mediocrity that is so fundamental to science, but is one of the most contentious and difficult scientific concepts for people to grasp, according to the biologist P. Z. Myers, who explains its meaning this way:

> The mediocrity principle simply states that you aren't special. The universe does not revolve around you.... Most of what happens in the world is just a consequence of natural, universal laws—laws that apply everywhere and to

everything, with no special exemptions or amplifications for your benefit.[6]

In fact, we humans aren't even as special relative to other animals as many of us would like to believe. In *Are We Smart Enough to Know How Smart Animals Are?*, Frans de Waal, a primatologist and professor of psychology at Emory University, explains that despite centuries of the presumed superiority of humans, science is beginning to reveal advanced cognitive skills among several animal species. "We are not the only intelligent life on earth," according to de Waal.[7]

---

### Reflection Time

We believe that a mindset of Humility underlies all the SMA Skills and the key behaviors necessary to excel at those skills. Think about it:

How can you be a good critical or innovative thinker or a good collaborator if it's "all about you"?

How can you truly be open-minded and willing to stress-test your hypotheses, and experiment, fail, and learn from mistakes, if you can't be honest about your strengths, weaknesses, abilities, and achievements?

How can you effectively understand and consider different views or collaborate if you're self-absorbed, don't view other perspectives as valuable, and thus are unable to quiet your ego and really listen to people?

---

Humility underlies and can enable humans to excel at every one of the NewSmart Behaviors and SMA Skills. You'll be able to see that more clearly when we describe the behaviors in detail in Part 2. In sum:

Humility includes a strength to "forget the self," which in turn fosters:

- Quieting Ego
- Reflective Listening
- Managing Self
- Otherness (emotionally connecting and relating to others)

Humility includes open-mindedness, a required state of mind for:

- Critical thinking
- Innovative thinking
- Creativity

Humility includes accepting our strengths, weaknesses, and mistakes, and keeping our abilities and accomplishments in perspective, which makes these tasks easier:

- Stress-testing our thinking
- Admitting when we don't know the answer
- Learning iteratively
- Managing Self (thinking and emotions)

Humility includes an appreciation for the value of other people, which enables:

- Empathy
- Relationship building
- Collaboration
- User-centric innovative thinking

We are not saying that a complete loss of self-interest or ambition is advisable. Certainly not. The problem is not in *being more successful* than others but in needing to prove that we're better/smarter/more special than others in order *to feel successful*, which leads to the kind of ego defensiveness that gets in our own way. It's that kind of excessive self-focus that's not in our long-term interest in the SMA. Instead, the outward focus that follows from a Humility mindset is what's in our best interest. Truly effective teamwork, collaboration, and innovation can't happen when we're defensive or when we're too tied up in looking or feeling superior to our colleagues, teammates, clients, or customers (big me). We must instead approach the SMA with Humility (big us).

| Big Me | Big Us |
|---|---|
| Ego defensive | Self-accurate |
| Self-focus | "Forget the self" |
| Big mouth | Big ears |
| Inwardness | Outwardness |

A side note about a common confusion between *modesty*, which means a lack of boastfulness, and humility: in many cases modesty is about social propriety rather than a person's actual disposition. Consider the self-deprecating person who downplays or refutes compliments, claiming that he or she isn't that good, or smart, or creative, or makes a fuss that whatever he or she did wasn't that hard or whatever. While on the surface such people are making a show of not thinking too highly of themselves, in actuality these kinds of statements are hyperfocused on the self. **Humility is often reflected in modesty, but the reverse is not necessarily true.**

## The Humility Advantage

It's vital that in the SMA, it's no longer all about you. You alone aren't special. That's harsh and would make the self-esteem proponents cringe, but, in the SMA, winners will be those people who are less self-absorbed, because we need to open our minds, accept our mistakes and weaknesses, focus outward, and enlist others to help us think, innovate, create, and continually learn. Success will come to those who value building relationships, and that in turn requires that we aren't tied up in excessive self-interest but willing to emotionally engage, empathize, and be generous with and willing to help others.

Adam Grant, a professor of management and psychology at the Wharton School of the University of Pennsylvania, argues in his book *Give and Take: Why Helping Others Drives Our Success* that "giving"—helping others regardless of what you get in return (i.e., generosity)—is the foundation of effective collaboration, innovation, quality improvement, and service excellence. One study out of the University of Arizona that Grant highlights in his book found higher rates of giving were predictive of higher unit profitability, productivity, efficiency, and customer satisfaction, and lower costs and turnover rates.[8] Humility has been discussed in leading business books like the 2001 landmark bestseller by Jim Collins, *Good to Great: Why Some Companies Make the Leap ... and Others Don't.* In his research Collins found that a key attribute of leaders of "good to great" companies was "a paradoxical blend of personal humility and professional will."[9]

The business world and media sat up and took notice, and several other studies have since confirmed that employees who identify leaders and managers as more humble, empathic, and compassionate also report greater commitment and engagement.[10] Moreover, much has been written about the need for organizations to be more adaptive and flexible in order to remain competitive in an increasingly dynamic global economy, and that the old hierarchical organizational model in which "often wrong but never in doubt" leaders and managers rule is outdated.[11] Humility has emerged as a key leadership theme during Ed's research into high-performance companies and exemplar learning organizations for his previous books. For example, when Ed asked Jim Quinn, then president of Tiffany & Co., for one word to describe his organization in an interview a few years ago, he said, "Humility. There is only one star here and it is Tiffany."[12]

Ray Dalio explained humility to Ed as understanding that "we all are dumb shits,"[13] a fact often exposed at Bridgewater through a company policy called Radical Transparency. Included in that policy is the highly unusual practice of filming all meetings for later review by anyone at the firm and the use of employee scorecards of strengths and weaknesses that are digitally accessible to the whole company. Bridgewater employees are expected to regularly log performance ratings of each other through proprietary iPad apps. Dalio subjects himself to this same humbling, regular feedback.[14]

Scott Cook, cofounder of Intuit, has said that "the most important person to be learning and growing in a company is the CEO" and that leaders must find a way to get feedback with the "unvarnished truth." He also walks the talk, engaging in 360-degree performance reviews and disclosing his need for "deferred maintenance."[15] Brad Smith, Intuit's CEO, has also been vocal about the need for leaders, including himself, to lose their egos and be good at "not knowing" to fuel innovation. He has stated that the "modern day Caesar" type of manager who commands and controls decision making must be buried in order to give employees the autonomy to engage in what Intuit calls Rapid Experimentation—testing ideas quickly and cheaply to allow the best ones to rise to the top.[16]

In his book *Work Rules! Insights from Inside Google That Will Transform How You Live and Lead,* Laszlo Bock, Google's former senior vice president of people operations, identified "humility" as one of Google's top hiring requirements.[17] What he means by humility is the ability "to step back and embrace the better ideas of others," as well as "intellectual humility," without which, he explained, "you are unable to learn," particularly from failure.[18] The reason you can't learn from failure is that without humility, Bock said, you're stuck in a false attribution/blame mindset: "If something good happens, it's because I'm a genius. If something bad happens, it's because someone's an idiot or I didn't get the resources or the market moved."[19]

Humility is also vital in Google's leadership and management practices. Bock explains that the company operates as an idea meritocracy where data, not the HiPPO (highest-paid person's opinion), drive decisions. Google discourages hierarchy, and all employees have an obligation to dissent if they disagree. Keeping quiet is countercultural. Google believes that employees will find work more meaningful if they have a "voice."[20]

Catmull's book on the inside story of Pixar is similarly full of references to the vital role humility has played in the company's success. In *Creativity, Inc.* Catmull summed up how an organization's leaders can embrace and role-model this approach when he said:

I believe the best managers acknowledge and make room for what they do not know—not just because humility is a virtue but because until one adopts that mindset, the most striking breakthroughs cannot occur. I believe that managers must loosen the controls, not tighten them. They must accept risk; they must trust the people they work with and strive to clear the path for them; and always, they must pay attention to and engage with anything that creates fear. Moreover, successful leaders embrace the reality that their models may be wrong or incomplete. Only when we admit what we don't know can we ever hope to learn it.[21]

Perhaps the most powerful example of the power of Humility in achieving the highest levels of human performance and collaboration is provided by the elite special forces of the US military. It's easy to understand why the members of special forces would excel at the ability to "forget the self" in favor of the safety and success of the group and mission, but this extends to leadership as well. In the well-received leadership book *Extreme Ownership*, two former US Navy SEALs explain that implementing the kind of extreme ownership leadership practiced by the SEALs "requires checking your ego and operating with a high degree of humility."[22]

Humility is the gateway to human excellence in the SMA. We believe that it's necessary in order to excel at the foundational NewSmart Behaviors that we discuss in Part 2, which underlie the highest levels of thinking, learning, and emotionally engaging with others—the SMA Skills. As such, we believe that Humility is the real hero of our story. We hope that you will deeply and seriously consider adopting Humility as your mindset.

## Reflection Time

Why would a mindset of Humility be so important in doing the kinds of critical and innovating thinking that are needed at Bridge-water Associates?

Why would a mindset of Humility be so important at Google?

Why would a mindset of Humility be so important at Pixar?

Why would a mindset of Humility be so important to the Navy SEALs?

What does Humility mean to you now?

Do you think Humility will help or hinder your future success? Why? How could you test that belief?

# Part 2

# NewSmart Behaviors

In the next four chapters, we focus on "how to" perform four of the most foundational behaviors that underlie the SMA Skills: **Quieting Ego, Managing Self, Reflective Listening,** and **Otherness.** As we mentioned earlier, people are more inclined to change their behavior if they first change their personal mental model—their views of self and the world—in a manner that supports those new behaviors. In other words, beliefs drive behaviors, and we believe that accepting the NewSmart definition and the Humility mindset will enable you to embrace the NewSmart Behaviors that underlie the SMA Skills.

But good intentions are not enough. You must slow down and make daily, thoughtful choices and exert effort to engage in the behaviors that will allow you to develop the skills you'll need to survive and thrive. Behaviors are measurable—and measuring yourself and holding yourself accountable are necessary for improvement. And to be good at any behavior, you must know *what* to do, understand *how* to do it, and have the motivation to do it. And you have to "do it" consistently in an excellent manner. The more you do that, the easier it becomes. Walter Mischel, a psychologist and the author of *The Marshmallow Test: Mastering Self-Control*, explains the reinforcing nature of practicing behaviors this way: "If we persist ... the gratification that our new behavior produces will help sustain it: the new behavior itself becomes valued, no longer a burden but a source of satisfaction and self-confidence. As with all efforts to change long-standing patterns and learn new ones ... the prescription is to 'practice, practice, practice' until it becomes automatic and intrinsically rewarding."[1]

In these chapters we offer ideas, templates, processes, and tips gathered from science, our field research, our work with managers and leaders, and our own experiences and experiments in trying to improve our NewSmart Behaviors. And we discuss in detail how these behaviors, illustrated in the diagram below, build on as well as reinforce and interact with each other to help you perform the SMA Skills.

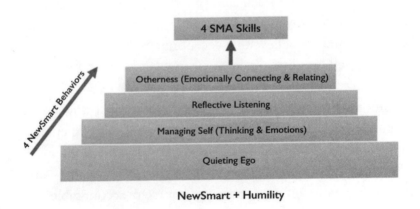

We settled on these particular behaviors by reverse engineering the four SMA Skills to determine the most fundamental common behaviors underlying them, based on researching hundreds of academic articles and over forty-five leading books about those four skills. Other behaviors are important, too, but we believe that these four behaviors are foundational. Another fundamental concept that we discuss in Part 2 is *choice*. In working through the content of this book in workshops and classrooms, it became apparent to us that many people don't fully understand how much of our behavior as humans is a result of a choice. Too many times, we operate on autopilot or react or act reflexively without intention. For example, most of us have the choice to do the following throughout the day:

1. Think and behave with focus, deliberation, and intention or operate on autopilot
2. Be wholly present in the moment or let anxieties and rumination distract us
3. Respond to our fears and insecurities in a particular way
4. Listen to others with a nonjudgmental, quiet mind (or not)
5. Translate feelings into behaviors (or not)
6. Act defensively (or not)
7. Connect with people (or not)

Please take a moment and think about what other choices you would add to that list.

We believe that the choices we make—how we think, how we listen, how we manage our ego and fears, and how we connect and relate—will determine our ability to thrive in the SMA. In her wonderful book *Positivity: Groundbreaking Research Reveals How to Embrace the Hidden Strength of Positive Emotions, Overcome Negativity, and Thrive*, Barbara Fredrickson quotes this story from Cherokee folklore:

> One evening an old Cherokee told his grandson about a battle that goes on inside us all. He said, "My son, the battle is between two wolves inside us all. One is Evil. It is anger, envy, jealousy, sorrow, regret, greed, arrogance, self-pity, guilt, resentment, inferiority, lies, false pride, superiority, and ego. The other is Good. It is joy, peace, love, hope, serenity, humility, kindness, benevolence, empathy, generosity, truth, compassion, and faith." The grandson thought about it for a minute and then asked: "Which wolf wins?" The old Cherokee simply replied, "The one you feed."[2]

We all have limited resources, both physical and psychological. If we expend most of our energy on being self-focused, protecting our egos, and trying to look smarter than everyone else in the room, then we won't have enough energy to do the tough work of thinking critically and innovatively and focusing on and really listening to others, which we know is the key to better learning, thinking, and relating.

Although we discuss each of the four NewSmart Behaviors separately, they are not in fact distinct steps on the road to developing SMA Skills but are in many ways overlapping and mutually reinforcing. For example, Quieting Ego helps us manage our emotions and thinking and vice versa. Reflective Listening is both aided by and helps enable a quiet ego. Otherness—emotionally connecting and relating to others—requires and is made possible by Reflective Listening. That being said, we have found that for many people, these behaviors build on each other in the order presented in the diagram above. As such, in chapters 4–7 and in the NewSmart Behaviors Assessment in chapter 8, we address the behaviors in that order.

# 4

# Quieting Ego

Quieting Ego is how we can deliberately work to reduce our reflexive emotional defensiveness; have empathy and open-mindedness; engage in Reflective Listening; and proactively seek other people's feedback and perspectives to stress-test our own thinking. Quieting Ego is a way of practicing and operationalizing Humility. To quiet our ego is to perceive others and the world without filtering everything through a self-focused lens and to tamp down on negative or self-protective "inner talk" that is driven consciously or subconsciously by our fears and insecurities. Inner talk is part of our story of how we perceive the world. In many cases those perceptions are untrue, and this tendency to self-focus and distort reality negatively affects our behavior, thinking, and ability to relate to and engage with others.

Take a moment to think about your inner talk. We all have fears and insecurities, and we all want to be accepted, appreciated, and loved; however, we differ in the degree and the manner in which we choose to deal with our fears and insecurities. The purpose of quieting that self-focused inner talk is to be more open to perceiving the world as it really is—not as we wish or have rationalized it to be—and this clearer, more open and accurate reception is necessary to be highly proficient at the four SMA Skills.

## Mindfulness

We have found that the most effective way to quiet our ego is through practicing mindfulness. Most of us by now are familiar with the term *mindfulness*. Jon Kabat-Zinn may be credited, at least in part, with making mindfulness part of mainstream medicine thanks to scientifically proven outcomes. In 1979 he founded the Stress Reduction Clinic and the Center for Mindfulness in Medicine, Health Care, and Society at the University of Massachusetts Medical School. Kabat-Zinn describes mindfulness as "paying attention in a particular way: on purpose, in the present moment, and nonjudgmentally."[3] According to a study by the Harvard psychologists Matthew Killingsworth and Daniel Gilbert, most adults spend only about 50 percent of their time in the present moment.[4]

Quieting Ego through mindfulness results in heightened attention and awareness to experience and reality that is open and receptive without bias or distortion. It's brutal honesty without the brutality. That sounds simple, but of course achieving nonjudgmental mindfulness is anything but simple. Why? Because, as we've already explained, we're so judgmental by nature. Because our egos get in the way of seeing things objectively. Because we're too concerned with defending our egos and with evaluating ourselves to just "be" and just "see" clearly. Because we're prone to thinking and reacting reflexively rather than deliberately. It's something we humans have been struggling with for centuries. As William James wrote in his renowned *Principles of Psychology* over a hundred years ago: "Voluntarily bringing back a wandering attention, over and over again, is the very root of judgment, character and will."[5]

Mindfulness is a state of awareness, but many people associate it with the practice of meditation. Kabat-Zinn helped show that the practice of mindfulness through meditation can help reduce stress and help people cope with pain, illness, and anxiety. Subsequent scientific studies of mindfulness over the last thirty years have shown that practicing it through meditation can change the physical structure of the brain and improve cognitive functioning directly by increasing working memory and attention and indirectly by helping us regulate emotions and reduce stress and anxiety.[6]

Another recent study of 327 undergraduates found that those who rated higher for mindfulness on the Mindful Attention Awareness Scale also had more resilience as rated by the Connor-Davidson Resilience Scale.[7] In other words, people who are better able to stay focused on the present moment in a nonjudgmental way are also better able to cope with difficult thoughts and emotions without becoming overwhelmed or shutting down (emotionally). That means mindfulness is associated with better management of uncertainty and challenge and bouncing back from failures and setbacks, all of which is crucial for innovation in the SMA.

## Mindfulness meditation in practice

Meditation is one way to improve mindfulness, to quiet our egos, and to behave with humility, but we're not just talking about the kind of rigorous, daily meditation practices of the monks. One study showed improvements on cognitive testing from participants after only four days of training in mindfulness exercises for twenty minutes a day. Kabat-Zinn's mindfulness meditation program is now widely used in health centers throughout the world. There are different kinds of meditation practice. All involve putting yourself in a relaxed position and focusing your attention on one thing. That one thing can be your breath, your body, a part of your body, or positive feelings such as loving kindness, gratitude, or compassion. And when your mind does its usual thing of bringing stuff into your consciousness, you experience it in a detached way and return your focus to the breath or your body, and so forth. Eventually you train yourself to control what you attend to, and you learn not to self-identify with all your thoughts or feelings.

Over time you begin to learn that you have an ability to choose whether to let the interrupting thoughts and feelings hijack your focused attention. The practice of mindfulness lets thoughts just pass through our mind. We do not have to identify with them or believe every one. We do not have to automatically practice "self-ing"—our tendency to put ourselves and our thoughts and feelings first. That choice is so powerful when it applies to opening up our minds to disconfirming data, to listening reflectively, and to emotionally connecting and relating to others. That choice is important when our mind wanders in important collaborations and when we start becoming defensive in response to feedback or anxious about failing. Mark Williams, a professor of clinical psychology at the University of Oxford and a well-known expert in this area, defined mindfulness this way in his book with Danny Penman, *Mindfulness: An Eight-Week Plan for Finding Peace in a Frantic World*:

You come to realize that thoughts come and go of their own accord; that *you* are not your thoughts. You can watch as they appear in your mind, seemingly from thin air, and watch again as they disappear, like soap bubbles bursting. You come to the profound understanding that thoughts and feelings (including negative ones) are transient. They come and go, and ultimately, you have a choice about whether to act on them or not.[8]

Williams believes that mindfulness takes us out of our dominant analytical "doing" mode and puts us in a "being" mode, experiencing what is in front of us with clarity. Visualize how this would work when you're listening to someone by just "being" in the listening mode without your mind judging or creating a response to what the other person is saying. How about when working with a team trying to be innovative or when solving a problem or creating something? What would it be like to just focus on "being" fully present with an

---

### Reflection Time

Mark Williams's quote is worth rereading and savoring. It can be personally transformative. He says that *you* are not your thoughts. He also says that thoughts and feelings (including negative ones) are *transient*, that they *come and go*, and that you have a *choice* of whether to act on them or not. What does that mean to you? Are you surprised? When I (Ed) began my mindfulness journey, I was surprised. I never really understood that all that went on inside my mind didn't have to be "me." Then, I learned it was just thoughts or emotions and that I had a choice to hold on to them or just let them float away.

What do *you* think? How does this feel to *you*?

---

open, uncluttered mind during brainstorming, exploring alternatives, or engaging with customers? Just "being" and trying
to sense reality clearly is much different than "doing" with a
personal agenda.

**"In mindfulness, we start to see the world as it is, not as
we expect it to be, how we want it to be, or what we fear it
might become,"** says Williams. Mindfulness teaches us how
to slow down our automaticity—our reflexive way of trying
to quickly interpret input so it fits with our existing beliefs.
Mindfulness practice is intended to develop cognitive clarity
and reduce our habitual way of confirmatory thinking that
tries to make things fit cohesively into our mental models and
our egocentricity.

Mindfulness is a way of "being good at not knowing,"
or having what Kabat-Zinn refers to as a "beginner's mind,"
which means being open-minded even if one has ideas, opinions, or expertise. Isn't that our goal? Doesn't critical thinking
require us to see things as they really are? Doesn't innovative
thinking and creativity require us to see things we don't usually see? In addition to thoughts, Quieting Ego through mindfulness also gives us the ability to view *feelings* as transient and
let them pass rather than cling to them. It can help us slow
down our inner machine (heart rate, pulse, and breathing) so
that we can be more calm and attentive in a way that we can
see the world without stress, anxiety, and automatically judging or being defensive. The scientific research on mindfulness
shows that the practice of mindfulness meditation can help
you do the following:[9]

1. Enhance your ability to regulate your attention.
2. Enhance your awareness of subtle body activities.

3. Regulate your emotions.
4. Be less self-absorbed and self-centered.
5. Reduce emotional defensiveness and self-identification.
6. Improve immune function.
7. Increase positive emotions and decrease negative emotions.
8. Reduce reactivity to inner experiences.
9. Enhance sensory awareness without judgment.
10. Enhance cognitive functioning.
11. Decrease heart rate, blood pressure, and breathing rate.
12. Be calm.
13. Reduce activity in the amygdala—the area of the brain. involved in responding to emotional stimuli (e.g., anxiety and fear).

I (Ed) began my exploration of mindfulness meditation in 2011, when it was getting some press in the business world. I had read about meditation several times before then, and I found Eastern philosophy quite interesting. But I hadn't tried it. I had an image of someone sitting in an uncomfortable position on a pillow chanting meaningless words. I was not open-minded about it.

It was Ray Dalio who inspired me to take a harder look at mindfulness meditation in 2013. He believed that meditation was foundational to his approach to life and how he conducted his business. Dalio himself has said that the Beatles' trips to India inspired him to begin trying meditation in his early adult years. Today he meditates at least twenty minutes a day, unless, as he has said publicly, it's going to be a tough day, in which case he meditates for forty minutes. The more I studied Bridgewater Associates, the more convinced I became that

Dalio designed its culture and processes based on the science of learning and that he was trying to help his people mitigate ego and fear. He was doing things based on science. He was a thoughtful person. He had a quiet ego.

---

### Reflection Time

What do you think about Mindfulness Meditation? What do you think about the scientific research findings about the benefits of meditation?

How do those research findings relate to having a quiet ego?

---

I had learned from doing research inside successful companies that one has to be on guard against people who talk a good game—they may say it, but they don't behave it. So I have trained myself to approach successful business leaders with skepticism and to be on guard against being sold a bill of goods. I had personal phone calls with Dalio; I watched hours of his work conversations on film (recall that all meetings at Bridgewater are recorded); and over a two-day visit to the company, I spent time with him personally and observed how he behaved with others in various Bridgewater meetings. I became convinced that Dalio was real, that he "walked the talk," and that he lived what he wrote in his *Principles*. He spoke so highly of meditation's positive effects that I made a choice to give it a try.

I started with Kabat-Zinn's book *Mindfulness for Beginners* and a CD of his that Lili Powell, a friend and colleague who practices and teaches mindfulness, gave me. I struggled until I found the right position, which for me was lying down on my exercise mat. I focused on my breathing and was bombarded with a stream of thoughts, including my mind critiquing my meditation performance. If I turned my attention to some thought that popped up, then my mind started kicking me in my butt, telling me that I wasn't supposed to do that while meditating. My mind was doing what our minds do well— dominating us with chatter.

I was impatient in that I erroneously thought that the parade of thoughts in my head would stop easily or quickly. I was missing something. So I did some more research and found Mark Williams's book, with a foreword by Kabat-Zinn. Williams had an eight-week plan. At that stage of my practice, I spent too much time on each thought before controlling my attention by returning my focus to my breath. I learned that what I was experiencing was normal for a beginner and that it takes a lot of practice to reach the point of having periods of stillness in your mind.

So I learned the drill: be aware of the uninvited thought … tell it to move on like a soap bubble … and intentionally return my focus to my breathing. In the beginning I did that for five minutes a day. That was my limit. But I kept with it, and after some time I moved up to ten minutes per day. I also experimented with focusing on my body—doing a body scan starting with my toes and going slowly up my body. And I tried to focus on my heartbeat. I had not read that anywhere, but for some reason it seemed right. Focusing on my heartbeat led me to the next stage.

One morning about two months into the practice, I focused on my heartbeat, and after becoming still and quiet, I felt it for the first time, pulsing in one of my teeth. I know it sounds weird, but the clarity and intensity of my focus and the still-ness of my mind made it feel like my heart was beating inside that tooth. That was a breakthrough for me because it was my longest period of having a quiet mind up until that point. It was really quite cool. That motivated me to keep going. From a minimum of ten minutes, I edged it up slowly until I reached fifteen minutes a day. Then things got really interesting. I found that the stillness of my mind increased. Yes, my thoughts would interrupt my stillness, but I had learned to make them "move on" and return to my focus, decreasing the time I spent on each thought. I didn't let them take over my session. I didn't engage with them. And as I did that over time, those interfering thoughts became like soap bubbles floating away quickly.

After a year, I started experiencing something else remarkable. After a good session, I always stretch and sit on my mat with legs crossed and bent over so my stomach crunches. Several times when I finished that exercise I would have a new idea pop into my head out of nowhere that solved a problem I was working on: a new way to teach, a new idea for an article, or simply a new mental connection. These new ideas still just happen every once in a while, which for me is the icing on the cake.

I am now up to practicing mindfulness for about thirty minutes a day. I have also adopted a program of doing mini-sessions for two or three minutes or so during the day, if I feel like my mind and body are going too fast. That took a while to perfect, but now I can calm myself pretty well in a mini-session, which I do if I'm going to a meeting that may be stressful or contentious or in which there will be lots of people who are self-centered and competing for airtime.

Through all of this I learned that I have a choice as to whether I let my thoughts or emotions define or control me.

Either I can just let them pass and not engage with them, or I can decide to engage. Previously, I always engaged. I have learned that stillness in your mind opens you up to really being present. I have also learned that stillness in my mind doesn't mean my unconscious mind isn't working, because after stillness, new stuff pops into my mind that is for me creative or innovative thinking. It has materially lowered my heart rate and made me more aware of what's going in my body, making me more sensitive to becoming emotionally defensive or hyperreactive. I'm calmer in general and in a different place now.

Mindfulness meditation more than anything I have done has quieted my ego and allowed me to embrace Humility, and that has helped me become a better thinker, listener, relator, and collaborator. Mindfulness meditation has slowed me down, allowing me to be calmly present when I talk to people, and that has led to better meetings and results. It has made me appreciate the power of slowing down in a world where everyone is trying to do more and more faster and faster with fewer and fewer resources. I know it sounds crazy, but for me slowing down has made me more productive because when I'm engaged, I'm more fully engaged. I find myself getting into a state of "flow" more often with tasks or conversation. I'm now very sensitive to my heart rate, to the speed of my breathing, to my body temperature, and to the pace of thoughts going through my mind. When I get going too fast, I make mistakes and I revert back to a more inner focus—a big me orientation—that results in higher emotional reactivity, an inclination to defend myself, and more closed-mindedness.

I'm grateful to Ray Dalio for helping me begin my mindfulness meditation journey. It has been transformative for me.

It has helped me quiet my ego. The science is clear about its benefits, and my personal experience confirms that. I invite you to consider it. Thank you, Ray.

---

### Reflection Time

How do you know if you're being mindful?

What do you think of the research finding that 50 percent of the time people are not mindful?

---

## Daily Quieting Ego reminders

Practicing meditation can help make mindfulness more of a habit, but there are other ways you can choose to quiet your ego on the spot. I (Ed) decided that I required a daily reminder to be aware of the need to quiet my ego and be more "other" focused. I woke up one morning with the idea that I would sign all my emails as "ed," not "Ed." A small step, but it had meaning for me. To me, it was my way to accept the mediocrity principle that we discussed in chapter 3. I'm just one of the billions of humans on this planet, and I'm not worthy of being a legend in my own mind. It was my way to remind myself many times a day that "it's not all about me" and that I'm just a little player in a big world. I am little "ed," not big "Ed." I expect that some of you may think that this is weird. I'm not advocating that you copy me. You may find your own Quieting Ego reminders.

In the beginning, signing my name "ed" had another, unexpected impact. It caused me to reread my emails to check for tone, whether I had been a positive force and whether I tried to connect and relate to the person I was writing to before I took positions or got into a "telling" mode right off the bat.

Did I use a greeting and address the person by name? Did I try to leave people in a good place? I continue those practices today. That small step slows me down to focus on the messages I'm sending, not just the words. It helps keep me from being on autopilot. It also reflects the communication research done by Jane Dutton, a professor of business administration and psychology at the University of Michigan's Ross School of Business. Dutton's research shows that more than 85 percent of a message we communicate to others is conveyed not in the words but in the tone and manner in which they are delivered.

Another daily step I began taking before meetings was to pause, take a few deep breaths to calm myself, and then say to myself several times: "I am not my ideas"; "My mental models are not reality"; and "This is not all about me." Now I try to be in a good place at the start of every meeting. I strive to be present with an open mind and to really listen to others. And I started grading myself after each meeting by mentally replaying the meeting, with the goal of becoming more aware of how I felt at those times when I did become defensive or too argumentative, or I stopped listening. I'm looking for triggers such as my pulse beating faster or my face feeling warmer or my body tensing up or my leaning forward toward the speaker—getting ready to "attack." That has helped me.

I have to be honest with you. It felt awkward, at first, to write about myself in the context of Quieting Ego. I had serious reservations. I decided to do it because over the last few years so many people expressed appreciation for my vulnerability in talking about personal challenges in my last book and in my consulting workshops. I'm being vulnerable here too … trying not to listen to my inner talk that wonders whether you'll like me or whether you'll think that I'm an arrogant person. I have rejected those insecurities and fears because I know deep down that my reason for detailing my personal story is to share my experience and to invite you to consider the science of Quieting Ego through mindfulness meditation and daily reminders that you choose. It still feels weird, but I reminded myself during every draft of this book that I'm not my feelings. I have a choice as to whether they dictate my behavior.

### Practicing gratitude

Another way to practice Quieting Ego is through gratitude. Studies of gratitude have discovered wide-ranging physical and psychological benefits associated with it, including immune system improvement, lower blood pressure, increased and longer-lasting positivity, and decreased stress, anxiety, and depression. A more recent study showed that gratitude and Humility are mutually reinforcing.[10] You can see how taking the time to thank others for helping you or making your life better or easier is important because it requires you to focus on the value of others. Gratitude can open us up to "otherness"—being less inner-focused and more open to others—but just like mindfulness meditation, you have to practice it.

You can practice gratitude by regularly writing down or pausing to reflect on what you're thankful for in a daily physical or mental journal. You can also practice gratitude by asking people if they're in a good place after a meeting or thanking them for a good meeting and for their generosity in giving time to you.

Think about someone who has had a big positive impact on your life. How does thinking about them make you feel? Does it help you feel that "it's not all about me"?

> ### Reflection Time
>
> Did you say "thank you" to someone yesterday for helping you or doing something well?
>
> How often do you thank your friends, significant others, children, and so forth for being there for you and being part of your life?

Note that for purposes of Quieting Ego through practicing gratitude, we aren't just talking about pausing to reflect on how good you have it. That may lead to more positivity and happiness, as research suggests it does, but it's also self-focused, or the "selfish side of gratitude," as Barbara Ehrenreich points out in a *New York Times* op-ed.[11] Putting the focus instead on how valuable and helpful others are to you—thanking them verbally or in writing—has the further effect of helping us adopt an appreciation of the importance of others in our life, which can not only increase our sense of well-being but also, and more important for thriving in the SMA, lessen our self-absorption and quiet our egos, thus improving our thinking, learning, and relationship building.

> ### Reflection Time
>
> How would you describe a quiet ego?
>
> How would Quieting Ego help you excel at critical thinking?
>
> How would Quieting Ego help you excel at creative or innovative thinking?
>
> How would Quieting Ego help you excel at emotionally engaging and collaborating with others?

# 5

# Managing Self:
# Thinking and Emotions

Managing Self—our emotions and thinking—aids us in engaging in the higher-level thinking and behavior required by SMA Skills. It's necessary to remain open-minded and be willing to test our beliefs and modify our points of view if presented with better data. It's also how we're able to overcome our fear of mistakes in order to take ownership of them and learn from them, and helps us more effectively relate to and collaborate with others.

Managing Self comes from the science of "self-regulation" and "self-control," which are broad psychological concepts that mean to monitor and manage one's emotions, thoughts, and behaviors. We all, of course, use self-regulation and emotional intelligence every day—when we decide to ignore distractions to do our work or recognize when we need to walk away from someone before we say something we'll regret. Some of us do these things a lot better than others, but all of us struggle to self-regulate our basic humanity—our biases, fears, insecurities, and natural fight-flee-or-freeze response to stress and anxiety. We all can do better, however, and increasingly we must—the SMA will require that we do so. Can you see how the tendency to "forget the self" and accept one's strengths, weaknesses, and mistakes, which comes with a mindset of Humility, puts you in a better frame of mind to manage your thinking and emotions?

## The Art and Science of Slowing Down

Let's talk first about a fundamental component of managing ourselves that is the simplest to understand but not always the simplest to do: **slowing down.** You might be thinking to yourself, slow down? That can't be right. I can't slow down: someone will look more efficient and productive than me, or I'll look lazy. Many people react this way when Ed introduces the concept of slowing down in his workshops because it's counterintuitive to the cultural pressures in this day and age of doing more and more, faster and faster, with fewer and fewer resources. Reflect a moment, though. Consider how slowing down is a significant component of all the SMA Skills and underlying behaviors. It's necessary to overcome the speedy automaticity of your thinking and behaving so that you can think and act deliberately, quiet your ego and your mind, and be willing to engage in system 2 thinking and really listen to and consider the perspectives of others.

Simply slowing down and deciding whether to choose to act quickly or instead take our time and engage deliberately in a situation is a first step in managing ourselves. Note that we're not advocating laziness, inefficiency, or a decrease in productivity, nor are we talking about maintaining a particular pace or speed for approaching work. What we're really talking about, again, is being mindful—slowing down to pay adequate attention and curb our reflexive cognitive and emotional ways. Our experience is that slowing down makes it easier to know when to switch from autopilot to intentional thinking mode, and it makes it easier to quiet one's ego and be more open-minded and less revved up and primed to emotionally defend, deny, or deflect different ideas or challenges to your thinking.

Slowing down often requires you to be aware of and sensitive to physical cues: the rate of your heartbeat; your body temperature; muscle tightness or tension; tightness in your stomach; your breathing pace; and feelings of being stressed, threatened, or emotionally reactive. Our physical state can be an early warning system. We need to pay attention to our body. Being sensitive to it gives you the opportunity to slow yourself down and to manage your thinking and your emotions.

## Managing How You Think

As you probably know, there are hundreds of books on thinking. They cover how to think critically, how to innovate using design-thinking tools, and how to boost creativity. There are also books on how to solve problems, how to do experiments using the scientific method, how to see insights that other people don't, how to think strategically. and on and on. Obviously, we can't go into these details here. At the end of this book, however, we provide a list of our favorite "how to" books. In this chapter, we want to share with you certain approaches and tools that we and others have found helpful. We intend for this discussion to inspire you to read more and to create your own thinking tools and processes that you can refer to daily.

Managing "how you think" is fundamental to becoming NewSmart and to defining yourself as a high-quality thinker willing to treat all your beliefs (not values) as hypotheses subject to stress tests and modification by better data (that is, to think like a good scientist). Amazon founder Jeff Bezos is reputed to have said that the difference between a good leader and a bad leader is that a good leader frequently stress-tests what's working in order to determine whether the assumptions underlying the business process or model are still valid. In other words, even if something isn't broken, one needs to frequently assess whether it will become broken soon because the facts you based your initial decision on may have changed.

Let's start with a question:

*How* do you think?

The question is intended to home in on the fact that you have a choice about whether and when to engage in system 2 deliberate thinking. It also brings to light the fact that *how* you think depends on the context. You may need to think critically, innovatively, creatively, or in some cases a combination of all three. Other questions that are helpful in exploring how people think include the following:

- Do you think differently depending on the purpose of your thinking?
- Do you have a specific process that you use to think critically?
- Do you have a specific process to think innovatively or creatively?

What's interesting to us, and we hope to you, is that people who are good at thinking do have such processes. Here are some ideas or steps to consider. Step one in managing how you think is to become sensitive to or aware of the circumstances under which you should slow down to engage in system 2 deliberate and intentional thinking.

---

### Reflection Time

Please think about it now: In what situations should you slow down to think deliberately and deeply? Some examples you might come up with are when you're

- trying to fix something that's broken or not working as you want
- making an important decision
- trying to understand something new
- trying to figure out how to get from point A to point B
- trying to understand another person's view
- brainstorming ideas
- experimenting
- analyzing numbers
- determining the pros and cons of alternatives
- figuring out what you believe and why
- participating in a debate
- critiquing your work or someone else's work or ideas

---

In these situations, a way to start managing your thinking and taking it up a notch, then, is to ask yourself these five questions:

1. What am I trying to do?
2. What is the purpose of my thinking?
3. What do I know?
4. What do I not know that I need to know?
5. How do I start?

## Thinking toolbox

After identifying the purpose—the what and why—of your thinking, you can then apply the right thinking or decision-making tools, processes, checklists, or templates for that particular purpose from a "thinking toolbox." Our thinking toolbox includes the following:[1]

- Root cause analysis: What is the real problem or the real cause? This analysis commonly uses the "Five Whys"—a process of asking why something happened and then asking why that answer happened repeatedly at least five times to get to the root cause.

- Unpacking of assumptions: What assumptions and inferences am I making? For each assumption, am I making further assumptions? What data do I have to support those assumptions? What facts would disprove those assumptions? Have I searched for those facts?[2]

- Critical thinking tools: Provided below.

- If-then thinking: If I do this, then what is likely to happen? What then could happen?

- Gary Klein's Recognition-Primed Decision Model: This model describes how experts assess situations and decide whether to go with their intuitive solution or not.[3]

- Gary Klein's PreMortem: Discussed in the next section.

- Gary Klein's Insight Process: Described in his book *Seeing What Others Don't: The Remarkable Ways We Gain Insights* (one of Ed's favorite books along with Kahneman's *Thinking, Fast and Slow*).[4]

- US Army After-Action Review (AAR): The AAR should become a daily tool for all of us in all aspects of our lives.

It's a great learning tool and simple to use. Ask yourself: What happened? Why did it happen? What worked well? What didn't work? Why? What will we do differently next time? This takes only a few minutes, and it helps you avoid making the same error or mistake again.[5]

- Design thinking: Try using tools from IDEO or Jeanne Liedtka's books.[6]

- A fast, low-risk experimental tool like Intuit's Rapid Experimentation process contained in its NEXT Tool, which is public on the company's website.[7]

- Twyla Tharp's creativity tools in *The Creative Habit: Learn It and Use It for Life*.[8]

- Creativitky tools in R. Keith Sawyer's book *Explaining Creativity: The Science of Human Innovation*.[9]

This list is not exclusive. Other tools by other people would work well, too. But we believe that this is a good starting point for you to create your own toolbox to help manage how you think.

### Klein's PreMortem

We find Gary Klein's PreMortem tool especially helpful.[10] Klein is a highly regarded research experimental psychologist who specializes in studying how people make decisions in real-world environments characterized by uncertainty and stress.[11] Ed loves the PreMortem and so do many of his consulting clients. The PreMortem process requires that before taking action on a big or important decision of any kind, you stop and visualize what failure would look like and then verbalize a list of all the possible reasons for such a failure. This process has two big benefits. One, it allows you to mitigate those risks before you act, and two, by verbalizing and thinking deeply about those risks, you can prime your mind to be on guard for them—and perhaps to see them if they happen to occur rather than being cognitively blind. Kahneman himself notes that the PreMortem is one of the few tools that helps mitigate confirmation bias.

### Critical thinking tools

Here are the two critical thinking tools that Ed uses in his workshops, with a short exercise at the end of each to help you "make meaning" of the tools.

#### Critical Thinking Purposes

1. Make good rational ("reasoned") and logical (based on facts) decisions while mitigating biases, emotional defenses, and downside risks.
2. Clearly define the issue or problem: Have you clearly defined it? Have you uncovered the root causes of the problem or issue?
3. Analyze your thinking: unpack assumptions and inferences. Why do you believe them?
4. Stress-test beliefs, assumptions, and inferences: Do you have enough credible data to justify your belief?
5. Uncover what you know and what you don't know: What do you need to know?
6. Be an unbiased detective ("just the facts"): Have you mitigated confirmation bias?
7. Illuminate and consider alternative points of view.
8. Weigh decision alternatives: consider first, second, and third consequences of potential actions and decisions.
9. Assess probability of being accurate.

10. Assess and mitigate material negative consequences (risks) that could occur if you're not accurate.
11. Learn from the results of your actions and decisions: What will you do differently next time?
12. Be aware of your emotions and intuitive feelings: use them to test your tentative decisions.

We suggest that you prioritize the Critical Thinking Purposes for daily use—what five are most important to you? We recommend that you take some time with this exercise, because to do it well you have to think deeply about each purpose. Having done this exercise with many people, we've found that it's much harder than it first appears because it forces you to prioritize by thinking critically about *how* you want to critically think. After considering these purposes, critical thinking may mean something different to you than it did before the exercise.

### Critical Thinking Questions

What do I think? Why do I believe that?

What assumptions am I making to get to that point?

What inferences am I making?

What facts must be true for that to be true? What factual support do I have? How credible are the sources of those facts?

Do I have enough (quantity) credible (quality) evidence to make those assumptions, inferences, or conclusions?

What facts would disprove my assumption, inference, or conclusion? Did I look for them?

What other interpretations or meaning can I draw from the facts?

What alternatives did I consider? What are the pros and cons of each? Why did I choose X?

Have I looked at the problem from different viewpoints?

Do I have enough data to make a decision?

Who disagrees with this course of action? Why? (Warning sign if no one disagrees.)

If I do this, what's likely to happen? What would that cause to happen? What could result then?

Is there something here that just doesn't make sense? Does it feel right?

Have we illuminated all the unacceptable risks of this decision or course of action?

What is the probability we're correct?

What are the big downsides if we're not correct? Have we mitigated or hedged the big downsides to nil?

Have we taken into account self-interest bias? Confirmation bias? Availability? Anchoring? Overconfidence? Loss aversion?

An exercise that could help you think more deeply about the Critical Thinking Questions is to prioritize them. What are the seven key questions you should ask yourself every day? It's hard but important to decide, because it should help you think more deeply about how to better manage critical thinking. Bridgewater Associates, for example, uses questions like this in every conversation in the company. We hope that this section will be a launch pad for thinking more deeply about "how" to think and "when" to take your thinking to a higher level. We hope that it has provided you with some ideas to consider in building your own thinking toolbox.

## Managing Emotions

We've discussed how ego and fear are the two big learning inhibitors and explored our reflexive tendency as humans to be emotionally defensive and self-protective. We've discussed how negative emotions can undermine our behavior and thinking and how positive emotions can improve them. Stress, anger, and anxiety can cause narrow-mindedness and the fight-flee-or-freeze syndrome. Remember that our evolutionary-based fight-flee-or-freeze response is helpful when you need to be in survival mode—to focus on escaping a predator, for example. It's not at all helpful when you need to engage in critical thinking, problem solving, innovative thinking outside the box, or designing experiments to learn.

Positive emotions, on the other hand, have been scientifically linked not just to higher health and well-being but also to broader attention, open-mindedness, deeper focus, and more flexible thinking, all of which underlie creativity and innovative thinking. Positive emotions also improve decision making and general cognitive processing. Negative emotions can and will be experienced, but they don't have to automatically drive behavior or automatically overtake our thinking. We have choice. Recall that mindfulness meditation helps us practice letting emotions pass through us without letting them consume us. Cognitive psychologists use the term *metacognition* to describe the process of managing our cognitive processes. We like to use the term *meta-emotions* to describe the process of managing our emotions. This process requires us to be mindful of and deliberately deal with emotions.

Again, paying attention to physical cues can be helpful. When you begin to feel your body speeding up or you feel stressed, anxious, or about to fight, flee, or freeze, how can you slow down your emotional reactivity? First, you breathe. Yes, you breathe, but in a deliberate, stress-reducing way. Are you willing to try something now before we continue? Please sit or stand still and take a deep breath inhaling slowly for four seconds, feeling your chest move up your body, and then slowly exhale over four seconds.

Do that four times slowly in a row.

How did it feel?

How do you feel after doing that as compared with before?

Most people say (and science supports) that you should feel calmer and more relaxed, as if weights have been lifted from your shoulders. Think about the power of that exercise, which takes less than a minute. Visualize yourself doing tjhat before every situation that may require higher-order thinking or emotionally engaging with others. Why not try it tomorrow before meetings that require your best performance?

## Managing emotions toolbox

After slowing down to pause and breathe, the next step in managing your emotions is to engage your cognitive processes. Recall that the mechanics of our emotions are inextricably intertwined with cognition in our minds, but we can use this to our advantage. Richard Davidson, a professor of psychology and psychiatry at the University of Wisconsin–Madison, explains: "These facts about the neural organization of emotion have important implications for understanding why our perceptions and thoughts are altered when we experience emotions. They also help to explain how we can use our cognitive machinery to intentionally regulate and transform our emotions."[12]

Here are five such ways we can leverage our "cognitive machinery" to manage our emotions and our reactions to them.

### 1. Psychological distancing

The self-control expert Walter Mischel explains that you can psychologically distance yourself from your negative emotions by imagining that you're a "fly on the wall."[13] You can look down at yourself and the situation as if it's happening to someone else in order to think about it impartially. Ray Dalio teaches a similar psychological distancing process to his team at Bridgewater Associates by advising them: "Get above yourself."[14]

### 2. Reframing

Another way to manage your emotions is to reframe a perceived negative situation. In her best-selling book *The Creative Habit*, Twyla Tharp refers to this as facing down your fears.[15] "No one starts a creative endeavor without a certain amount of fear; the key is to learn how to keep free-floating fears from paralyzing you before you've begun," says Tharp.[16] Likewise, Tom Kelley and David Kelley, IDEO's founders, explain in *Creative Confidence*, "Creative confidence depends on an absence of fear of failure and judgment."[17] For example, if you're feeling fearful or anxious, acknowledge exactly what that fear is and consider whether you can credibly look at the situation as a less fear-inducing one.

Can a performance review be recast as a learning opportunity?

Can a critique of your thinking be recast as an opportunity to get to the most accurate answer, thus helping you avoid a big mistake?

Can you logically reduce the magnitude of the situation's perceived potential harmful effect by downplaying the likelihood of something bad happening?

For example, if you're fearful of looking stupid in a brainstorming session, you could think about the fact that many people will come up with ideas that won't be good. Gregory Berns, a professor of neuroeconomics at Emory University, recommends these kinds of reframing techniques in *Iconoclast: A Neuroscientist Reveals How to Think Differently.*[18]

### 3. Positive memories

The third way to manage your emotions is to distract yourself from negative rumination by thinking about something positive that happened to you. This process is illustrated in a wonderful book by Bernard Roth, a Stanford engineering professor and "d.school" founder, called *The Achievement Habit: Stop Wishing, Start Doing, and Take Command of Your Life.* Roth discusses the work of the Harvard neurology professor Rudy Tanzi, who suggests four steps to slow down the automatic emotional impulses of our minds:

1. Stop yourself from acting in the manner dictated by the initial emotional reaction.
2. Take a deep breath.
3. Become aware of how you are feeling.
4. Recall a past event that made you happy or peaceful.

### 4. Positive self-talk

The relentless inner monologue that runs in our heads is often destructive. It's the internal voice that tells us "that was a stupid thing to say" or "this is not going to go well." We can, however, make a conscious effort to change this internal talk and make it more positive. Recent studies by Ethan Kross, a psychologist at the University of Michigan, have shown that using your own name when you "talk" to yourself makes a huge difference in achieving goals. For example, instead of thinking, "*I* can do this," it would be more effective for Katherine to say to herself, "*Katherine*, chill out. *You* can do this."[19] Rather than being egocentric, talking to yourself in the third person distances you from strong emotions in that moment. Similar to mindfulness, this kind of positive self-talk is a way to achieve detached awareness, making you a detached observer and offering yourself encouragement as if you were speaking to a friend.

### 5. If-then implementation plans

Mischel and two New York University professors, Peter Gollwitzer and Gabrielle Oettingen, have also found independently that a form of self-talk that involves "if-then" implementation plans can be effective for self-regulation. For example, you can be proactive in planning for anxiety-inducing or stressful situations by mentally visualizing how you would respond if someone challenged your thinking or is intent on making you look bad so they look good or becomes personally offensive in a work meeting. You can prepare a mental "if-then" implementation plan to proactively manage what you'll think and how you'll behave—if X happens, then I'll do Y. The key is to be specific, consistent, and mentally visualize yourself doing it. Practice it in your mind and out loud. Ingrain it in your mind. It's not enough to tell yourself *if* I get negative feedback, *then* I won't get upset, or *if* I fail, *then* I won't give up. As with most of our New Year's resolutions, explains Mischel in *The Marshmallow Test*, "we are wonderfully creative at making tepid commitments and then finding endless ways to get around them."[20]

---

### Reflection Time

Because fears of failure, uncertainty, embarrassment, rejection, and public ridicule are so inhibiting, we believe that all of us need to take ownership of our fears and use some of these tools to manage them as best we can. This is hard stuff—we know that. But it's so important. We invite you to reflect on these questions.

1. What tool or tools will you adopt to manage your emotions?
2. Will you start practicing them now and document your practice and your experiences using them?
3. Will you give yourself a couple of months to find what works best for you—to create your personal "if-then" plan?

---

### Emotional intelligence

It's not only managing our emotions and behavioral reactivity that's important for managing ourselves—it's also the ability to understand and react appropriately to other people's emotions—which together constitute emotional intelligence (EI). This is so very important because so much of the value-added work humans will do in the SMA will be done in small teams. We have discussed repeatedly how the best critical thinking and innovative thinking happens when thinking out loud with others, that is, small teams. The concept of EI was first advanced in 1990 by two academics at Yale University, Peter Salovey and J. D. Mayer. Unfortunately, since then, the science of EI has often been diluted and misinterpreted by the media and "pop psychology." Salovey and Mayer's definition and EI diagnostic tool, however, have stood the test of time. They define true emotional intelligence as "the ability to monitor one's own and others' feelings and emotions, to discriminate among them and to use this information to guide one's thinking and actions."[21] They expound on this definition in a four-part EI model that includes these abilities:

1. Perceive and differentiate emotions in self and others.
2. Use emotions to facilitate reasoning, aid judgment and memory processes, problem solve, communicate with others, and facilitate open-mindedness.
3. Understand and analyze the emotions of yourself and others.
4. Manage emotions.[22]

Sensitivity to other people's emotions has been found to be a key to effective collaboration. According to researchers from Carnegie Mellon's Tepper School of Business, MIT, and Union College, there is something called "collective intelligence" that explains a group's performance on a wide variety of tasks, and this "c factor" extends beyond the cognitive abilities of the group's individual members. In the experiments, groups of people were given various tasks like visual puzzles, negotiations, brainstorming, games, and complex rule-based design assignments.

The researchers found that collective intelligence not only extended beyond the individual intelligence (IQ) of group members but wasn't even correlated with individual intelligence levels at all. Instead, it was correlated with (1) the level of "social sensitivity" of group members (how well they perceived each other's emotions); (2) the equality in distribution of conversational turn-taking; and (3) the proportion of females in the group.[23] These factors held constant whether the teams were working face-to-face or online.[24] The positive correlation between the proportion of females in the group and the group's performance was a particularly surprising finding for the researchers, but what they discovered was that such results seemed to stem from the higher social sensitivity and turn-taking, on average, exhibited by the females.

Social sensitivity involves perceiving social cues and contexts in conversations, reading others' emotions, and empathy—the ability to put yourself in someone else's shoes in order to understand that person's perspective. Some of us are simply better at this than others, but all of us can improve. Slowing down and practicing mindfulness are two such ways. As with all the behaviors and skills we've discussed, it takes believing in the importance of empathy and then exercising choice, effort, and continuous practice. The lack of self-absorption that follows from Humility sets us up to engage in this kind of behavior. These findings should be reflected on because they're guideposts for effective collaboration. Success in the SMA will be a team effort. We believe that the most effective teams will have to be very effective collaborators.

Did you take a course on EI in school? Have you had EI training? Have you ever taken the Mayer-Salovey-Caruso Emotional Intelligence Test? We venture to guess that most readers have had little to no formal training in emotional intelligence. I (Ed) did not. As a result, my understanding of how emotions work and how they can be managed was almost nonexistent. I remember having arguments with my wife when we were much younger and how I would react emotionally and speak before thinking, which always made matters worse. She would say to me in response: "You know that emotions do not have to produce bad behaviors, don't you?" Well, to be honest, no, I didn't know that. If I had understood that, we probably would have had fewer arguments. Just as I had to learn that "I am not my ideas" and "my mental models are not reality," I had to learn that "I am not my emotions" and that I have a choice about how I respond to my feelings. I also have a choice over whether or not I slow down to consider the emotions and perspectives of others.

How do you become more sensitive to your own emotions? Science hasn't confirmed any universal physical characteristics of particular emotions;[25] however, there's clearly a connection between emotions and physical sensations. For example, some of us may feel nauseated when we're stressed, actually hot when we're angry, lethargic when we're sad, and energetic when we're happy. Consider whether you're beginning to experience a change in heart rate or body temperature or muscle tightness or feelings in your stomach. When you do notice something, try to label it and ask yourself what it is and why you might be feeling it. Ask yourself what might be happening externally that might be generating these feelings internally. Then accept your feelings before deciding what to do about them. Make a choice to engage with those feelings or let them pass. Using the five methods for managing fear that we discussed above, you can take the energy away from many negative emotions.

How about perceiving and responding to the emotions of others? Obviously, that's hard to do if you're absorbed with yourself. By now you should understand how vital it is to break out of that self-absorption to be an effective listener, relator, and collaborator. Having a mindset of Humility paves the way for "forgetting the self" in a way that makes paying attention to others organic. A way to practice this is to observe and be mindful of other people's body language and voice cues (tone and volume). Do they appear tense and fidgety or at peace with themselves? Are they making eye contact with you?

Others' emotions are being transmitted to you subconsciously, and when you're not self-absorbed in self-chatter or worrying about yourself, your intuition may give you the answer. If not, you can ask them: How are you feeling? Are you OK? Asking these questions shows caring and concern, and that in and of itself is a positive way to engage with others. EI and social sensitivity are so important in collaborating with others, and we cannot stress enough (although through much repetition, we've tried!) how important collaboration is to the SMA Skills.

---

### Reflection Time

Do you approach collaboration as a competition to see who wins or as a way to reach the best possible result regardless of whose idea wins?

Do you approach collaboration as a transactional process or a relational process—the difference being in how you value the people component?

---

# 6

# Reflective Listening

Reflective Listening is so important because it underlies all the SMA Skills. Why? Because your thinking and learning are limited by cognitive biases, emotional defensiveness, ego, and fear. You need, then, to truly listen to others to open your mind, push past your biases and mental models, and mitigate self-absorption in order to collaborate and build better relationships. We've already shown you the evidence that it's hard for any of us to critique our own thinking and truly think critically. We're just too wired to confirm what we already believe, and we feel too comfortable having a cohesive simple story of how our world works. We need to have thinking "partners" who force us to confront those biases, and we need to listen to them.

Likewise, we've shown that the most effective way to think innovatively is to think with others in small teams made up of people who have experiences and training different than us. Again, Reflective Listening is key to this kind of collaborating. And lastly, emotionally engaging with others requires Quieting Ego and having empathy, and that's both enabled and evidenced by listening reflectively to them. Reflective Listening indicates that you care about what the other person is saying, which builds the positive regard that leads to trusting relationships.

You may think that you're already a good listener. I (Ed) thought I was, but after truly digging into what it means to listen "reflectively," I realized that in fact I interrupted people frequently to finish their sentences or to put forth what I thought was the answer. I often was creating my response in my head while people were still talking. In fact, I was a very poor listener. I did everything wrong. I listened for cues as to whether I had an opening to make my point. I "read" people to accomplish my objectives. Most of my conversations had a personal objective. I was not into casual conversations that I considered idle chitchat. I looked at a conversation in most cases as a transaction—as a vehicle to accomplish something. My mind wandered a lot when I "listened." I got bored, and if I didn't actually interrupt, I fidgeted and lost eye contact with the speaker. Winning, looking smart, and telling what I "knew" to advance my cause were my only purposes in listening to others. Today it's embarrassing to write that. I was a piece of work. I was an awful listener at home and at work.

## Listening with a Quiet Ego and an Open Mind

Listening took on a different meaning for me one afternoon, when I was visiting my cognitive psychology mentor and dear friend Lyle E. Bourne Jr., a professor emeritus of psychology at the University of Colorado. I had just finished the manuscript for my previous book, and he asked me about my next project. I told him I was researching Humility and about how I believed it was foundational to being good at the skills that smart machines can't do well. After exploring that for a while,

I asked him: "What is the first word that comes to your mind when I say the word 'humility'?" His response was surprising to me. He said: "Listening." He told me that he believed being a good listener both requires and enables Humility. Until that point, I had not connected listening and Humility.

To be a good listener you have to be totally focused on the speaker with an open mind. You have to listen in a non-judgmental way, with the only goal being to try to understand what the other person is saying before you prepare and deliver your response. Good listeners ask questions to make sure that they understand before responding, or they paraphrase and repeat back what they believe that the person said and ask if they've understood correctly. Good listeners then reflect, and as Bourne explained to me, they "try on" the other person's idea to see how it would feel if they believed that, too. Taking the time to slow down and try on a new idea and see how it feels is what we mean by Reflective Listening. We believe it's a higher level of listening analogous to System 2 thinking. If you will, Reflective Listening is System 2 listening.

Bourne told me that listening is the way most of us learn. "Almost all learning comes from having conversations with others or oneself," he said. Some of the best work on "learning conversations" has been done by William Isaacs, a senior lecturer in the Leadership Center at the MIT Sloan School of Management. In *Dialogue: The Art of Thinking Together*, Isaacs explains that dialogue requires one to "slow down" and that "to listen is to develop an inner silence."[1] Note that this is exactly what mindfulness strives for—a quiet mind that can focus nonjudgmentally on what's real and true and present.

This kind of System 2 listening takes deliberate effort. It takes choice and effort to refrain from getting distracted or beginning to prepare your response while a person is still speaking. Isaacs says that our dominant perceiving sense is our eyes, and so we tend to process everything more at the speed of light than the slower speed of sound. Given the fact that, according to Dutton, we can cognitively process up to 600 words per minute, while most people speak at the rate of only 100–150 words a minute, you can see how much discipline it takes to truly listen.[2] But it's also pretty straightforward. According to Isaacs, "Perhaps the simplest and most potent practice for listening is simply to be still. By being still in ourselves, quieting the inner chatter of our minds, we can open up to a way of being present and listening that cuts through everything."[3]

---

### Reflection Time

Do you know any bad listeners? What do they do that makes them bad at listening? Do they interrupt you? Do they immediately begin telling you what they think? Do they make you feel listened to?

How would you rate yourself on Reflective Listening?

What are the key behaviors that you think are necessary to be an excellent reflective listener?

---

### The Art of Asking, Not Telling

Reflective Listening requires us not only to slow down in order to focus on what a speaker is saying but also to make a conscious choice to try to understand the speaker's viewpoint rather than rush to judgment. If we're truly listening reflectively, then perspective taking must come before evaluation, and to do that usually requires us to ask questions. Unfortunately, as Edgar Schein, a professor emeritus at the MIT Sloan

School of Management, so aptly states in *Humble Inquiry: The Gentle Art of Asking Instead of Telling,* we live in a culture not of asking but of "telling." He explains that telling conveys a hierarchical message in a conversation. If you go into telling mode before fully listening, understanding, or asking questions, you are in a sense telling the speaker that you're smarter and know more than he or she does. It makes sense that in our individualistic and competitive culture, knowledge workers have been primed to "tell" more than "ask," but clinging to that behavior is a significant impediment to performing SMA Skills.

Asking questions is also part of "being good at not knowing" in that you must be comfortable with the implication that you're asking because you don't know the answer. But you must ask the right kinds of questions. Isaacs says that an estimated 40 percent of all questions are really statements in disguise, another 40 percent are judgments in disguise, and only a small percentage of questions are genuine attempts to understand or learn from the speaker.[4]

---

### Reflection Time

Would you like to do an experiment? Tomorrow, after two or three times that you've engaged in listening to someone, mentally replay the conversation and compare how much time you spent telling versus asking questions.

---

Reflective Listening takes us back to the point we made at the beginning of Part 2 about choice. In every conversation, we have to make the choice to quiet our egos and be fully present; to reflect and try on the other person's ideas; to understand rather than confirm our own beliefs; and to ask real questions before advocating our position. And we have a choice to become emotionally defensive and react reflexively or not. Some of you are probably saying to yourselves: "I know all this. Listening is common sense!" Yes, this is not rocket science, but knowing that is not the same as doing it consistently, every day and in every conversation. Striving for personal excellence with respect to the NewSmart Behaviors is a high standard, requiring self-discipline and holding oneself accountable daily for the key components of the behaviors.

To thrive and excel at the SMA Skills requires most all of us to take these behaviors to a higher level. It's no different than being a great musician, artist, athlete, singer, painter, or innovator in that it takes hyperfocused, deliberate practice to be good at these skills. In this case, however, we're practicing to compete not against others but against our own reflexiveness, automaticity, and self-absorption. The SMA will make this kind of human development vital for each of us personally and will be a strategic necessity for organizations.

### Getting Ready to Listen Reflectively

We have found the following checklist helpful, for us as well as many of Ed's clients, in getting primed to focus on Reflective Listening before a meeting or conversation:

1. Is my mind clear? If not, take several deep, slow breaths.
2. Am I calm emotionally? If not, take a few more deep breaths, focusing on breathing in for four seconds and very, very slowly breathing out for four seconds.
3. Say to yourself a couple of times:
   - "I am not my ideas."
   - "It's not all about me."

- "Don't be defensive."
- "Ask questions before telling."
- "Don't interrupt."
- "Stay focused."
- "Critique ideas, not people."
- "Listen to understand, not to confirm."

Ed has found that not listening well is a common issue for busy managers and executives, so he includes a session on Reflective Listening in his company workshops. The morning after one such session, Ed began the next day's workshop with a typical check-in, allowing each participant to say a few words about the workshop so far. Several people talked. Then a gentleman who was a very senior leader spoke up. He expressed how he'd been shaken during the Reflective Listening session to learn how poorly he listened. He explained that later that evening, he'd reviewed the "Getting Ready to Listen Reflectively" checklist and kept it by the phone as he called his family. He said that he tried hard to listen during that conversation and thought he'd done a better job. Then he teared up in front of his colleagues and said: "That was the best conversation I have had with my wife and kids in years. In fact, my wife called me back to thank me." Ed in turn thanked him for having the courage to share that story with the group. It was a special moment for everyone in that workshop, and we hope that this story also demonstrates to you that the behaviors we're inviting you to consider embracing can benefit not just your work life but also your whole life.

---

### Reflection Time

Does being a good listener require you to quiet your ego? Why?

Do you agree that self-absorption and a tendency to be closed-minded or emotionally defensive would make it hard for you to be a good listener? Why do you believe that?

What are the key behaviors of a good reflective listener?

Why is Reflective Listening important in thinking critically?

Why is Reflective Listening important in creative and innovative thinking?

Why is Reflective Listening important in emotionally engaging and collaborating with others?

---

# 7

# Otherness: Emotionally Connecting and Relating to Others

By now, we hope that you understand how important it is to seek the help of others to thrive in the SMA. We need others because we can't think, innovate, or relate at our best alone. To relate to other people you first have to make a connection with them. It is by building a relationship over time that you build trust, and when you have caring trust, you have set the stage for the highest level of human engagement. Barbara Fredrickson explains that "good social relationships are a necessary condition for human flourishing. It is scientifically correct to say that nobody reaches his or her full potential in isolation."[1] In other words, we are all just "people who need people" in order to do our best thinking and learning—and doing that is critical for human excellence in the SMA.

So how do you get better at connecting and relating? It's quite obvious that connecting and relating to people is inhibited by arrogance, self-absorption, self-centeredness, not listening, closed-mindedness, lack of empathy, emotional defensiveness, and the ego protection and fear that flow from the Old Smart mental model. Accepting NewSmart and Humility as well as practicing Quieting Ego, Managing Self, and Reflective Listening lays the groundwork for relationship building with others. What else can you do to help yourself better focus on and connect with another person? Jane Dutton's landmark work on "high quality connections" is instructive here. For Dutton, there are five keys to connecting with others.[2] You have to

1. be present;
2. be genuine;
3. communicate affirmation;
4. listen effectively; and
5. communicate support.

We've already discussed being "present" and mindful in connection with Quieting Ego, but how do we *indicate* to another person that we're "present"? We do it with our words but also with our body language and emotions. So we face the person, make eye contact, genuinely smile, and open our hands and arms in a warmly inviting way. It's also the small external behaviors such as putting your phone or tablet down when people walk into your room or office, and turning toward them or getting up to invite them in while you're acknowledg-

---

### Reflection Time

How many times did you multitask yesterday while someone at work or home was talking to you?

Do you, as a matter of course, begin each engagement with a smile? (Remember, recognizing the importance of this is not the same as actually doing it.)

Do you look at people when they're talking with you?

Do you send positive or negative messages through your tone of voice?

---

ing them. This all seems so simple, right? But it's only the start of connecting, and it requires daily effort and choice.

Dutton's use of the term *genuine* is important. Being genuine means being authentic, honest, open, and vulnerable with other people. Sidney Jourard, who was a leading professor of the Humanistic psychology movement, explained another benefit of being genuine through his theory of self-disclosure in *The Transparent Self:* "It seems to be another fact that no man can come to know himself except as the outcome of disclosing himself to another."[3]

Being genuine is hard for many people in the workplace because they work in an environment that is not an emotionally positive, trusting one. In such cases, we're advocating being vulnerable not with people who may "harm" you but with people whom you deem trustworthy. The difficulty is that to build trust takes being genuine and vulnerable, so how do you know whether you can trust someone? Good question. Take small steps and see whether the other person reciprocates being genuine. All people need genuine human connections, so you hopefully already have them, but please understand that when you're building a trusting relationship, someone has to have the courage to take that first small step.

To "communicate affirmation," "listen effectively," and "communicate support" are all about showing positive regard for people as human beings by indicating your interest in them. In the workplace, these things are especially important if you hold a higher position. I (Ed) realized this in my last leadership role. I really liked getting to work early, because it's quiet and that's my most productive time of day. One morning I was walking toward the coffee area, engrossed in my seemingly very important thoughts and looking at the floor. In my periphery I noticed a young analyst who worked in one of my groups. I gave him a perfunctory nod and kept going, still deep in my thoughts. About two hours later, I got a call from that young man's boss who told me that he was about to lose the young man—his best analyst. When I asked why, the boss told me, "He doesn't believe he has a future here, because you don't like him."

Turns out that the young analyst interpreted brief encounters with me such as the one that morning as brush-offs. Oh my goodness. I explained that I was simply absorbed in my thinking, but I realized how important it was to this young man that I affirm his existence and at least be courteous. I immediately went to his cubicle, to the surprise of his work-mates, and apologized. I asked how could I make this right for him, and I worked hard to do so. Over the years he became a superstar high performer and worked with me on many projects. What did I learn? I learned the importance of being sensitive to those around me, and that even small interactions can have a big impact. That is why being mindful and emotionally sensitive are so important.

That was an early indication of my need to build better relationships at work, and endeavoring to do so has greatly improved my performance as well as the performance of those with whom I work. Relationship building is now becoming mission critical in the SMA, because innovative and critical thinking requires high-performing teams that collaborate well, and that simply doesn't happen unless the teammates have trusting relationships with each other. Trust doesn't just happen "poof." It takes hard work, and it requires slowing down and taking time to be genuine with and care about other people.

## Trust and Caring

How else to build trust and convey caring? False modesty and going through motions won't work. Research supports the fact that we're all pretty perceptive in determining insincerity and recognizing when people are only out for themselves, which just further undermines trust. Would you trust someone who always has to win or be right? Would you trust someone who views you as a competitor or a means to an end? Would you trust someone who is arrogant, self-promoting, a glory hog, and refuses to take ownership of his mistakes? Would you trust someone who, when challenged, becomes defensive and refuses to really engage?

Fredrickson describes the biochemistry and neuroscience of meaningful platonic relationships in *Love 2.0*. They require us, she said, to "escape our cocoon of self-absorption"[4]—a phrase that goes to the root of Humility that we've referred to frequently in this book. Relationship building also requires that we be willing to invest ourselves in the well-being of another solely for his or her sake and not because there's something in it for us, according to Fredrickson. It's something I (Ed) had to learn the hard way.

In my first leadership position in investment banking on Wall Street, I had high-producing teams. My style was very much "get it done." I led by example, never asked my people to do anything I wouldn't do myself, and believed that integrity, truthfulness, and treating all people with dignity were nonnegotiable. I told my team that if they produced, I would get them raises and bonuses and help them get promotions and/or further schooling. But what I didn't do was to get to know them as individuals. I didn't have time for chitchat. I didn't care about their personal lives. My relationships at work were transactional. I was good at reading emotions, but only if doing so pertained to getting work done. I became self-absorbed in my work, and in me. I was not meaningfully relating with anyone other than myself. That philosophy and behavior worked for me for six years until I got hit on the head by a proverbial boulder at home that opened my eyes there and at work.

During those same work years, I failed to turn off work mode when I got home. In my wife's words, I had become a business machine devoid of emotions and incapable of emotionally engaging and caring about her as a person. She told me that I needed to change, or she was out. It was then that I sought out a highly trained, well-respected executive coach. She helped me understand how meaningful relationships would add so much to my life and yield better outcomes at home and work. But it would require a lot of hard work by me.

She was right. I learned that if I took the time to really get to know my work teams individually over lunches and frequent personal check-ins, magical things would happen. It seemed the more they felt that I truly cared about them as human beings—not just as a means to my success—the more successful they were and in turn I was. It took time to connect and relate in the way that Dutton, Fredrickson, and Jourard talk about. It takes authentic caring because you can't fake this stuff.

The more I slowed down and took the time to get to know my team, the more we connected and the more I legitimately did care about them. The more honest I was with them about me personally, the more they trusted me and were open and honest with me about their personal hopes, dreams, fears, and so forth. They always knew that they had to perform, but now they also knew that I was there for them personally because I cared about them as people. And I really did. That took our work conversations to a higher level of openness, and that led to better thinking and innovation.

In his new book *Humble Consulting: How to Provide Real Help Faster*, Edgar Schein says that these types of more personal, open, and trusting work conversations overcome "professional distance" and lead to what he calls "Level 2 relationships."[5] Like him, we believe that we build such higher-quality relationships by investing time in really getting to know each other through humble inquiry and dialogue: asking open-ended personal questions, exhibiting an authentic caring attitude toward the other person, and disclosing personal thoughts and feelings.[6]

It's helpful to create a short list that you can use before a meeting to remind yourself how to connect and relate. Here's our list, which resulted from "making meaning" of the research. Your list may be different after making your own meaning.

1. Be really present.
2. Genuinely smile—a big smile.
3. Make eye contact.
4. Be positive.
5. Listen reflectively.
6. Stay fully present.
7. Do no harm.

---

### Reflection Time

How do you connect with people?

How do you know that you're connecting?

What do you think you need to do to emotionally relate to someone?

How do you demonstrate positive regard for others?

---

## Choose Words Wisely

In our work over the years, we've learned some other amazing tips on language that help us better connect and relate to others. For example, in Ed's executive education classes, the tool that helped the most to facilitate connecting with others in conversation was to say "Yes, and ..." instead of "Yes, but ..." That simple difference in phrasing changes conversations by making them less judgmental and hierarchical and can help reduce the other person's defensive reactions.

Ed learned this tool from a colleague, Jeanne Liedtka, a professor at the Darden School of Business and a highly regarded design thinking expert, who in turn had learned it from Darden ethics, strategy, and leadership professor Alec Horniman. While observing one of her classes over nine years ago, Ed recalls Liedtka making two memorable points to her executive students. First, she asked them to consider what would happen if they changed their "Yes, but ...." responses to "Yes, and ..." ones. Second, she said something that's central to excelling at the SMA Skills: "We all would be much better off at work and at home if we treated everything we believed as a hypothesis to be tested."

The "Yes, and …" point applies as well to our penchant for thinking in dichotomies. Many of us often think that everything is either *X* or *Y*. Most dichotomies, however, are false, because most things exist along a continuum. In *The Achievement Habit* Bernard Roth shared some other language tips. He advises using "want to" instead of "have to" and to use "won't" instead of "can't," because in each case the former emphasizes that you have the power of choice. Similarly, we learned from Ray Dalio to say "I believe" instead of "I think," in order to recognize that our beliefs are subject to critical stress-testing by others and that we may not be thinking clearly. Lastly, going back to the discussion of gratitude, you can't thank enough people enough of the time. Well, maybe you can, but few of us are that thoughtful.

# 8

# Your NewSmart Behaviors
# Assessment Tool

In chapters 4–7 we presented the four NewSmart Behaviors that we believe underlie the higher-level thinking and emotional engagement skills that humans will need to master in order to thrive in the SMA. Here we present a tool for you to assess your strengths and weaknesses with respect to those NewSmart Behaviors. The assessment reflects that each behavior requires you to excel at many different sub-behaviors or component behavioral parts. For example, Reflective Listening includes paying attention to a speaker's body language and not interrupting. The assessment asks how often you engage in these various sub-behaviors on a scale of 1 to 5. For most questions, the higher your score, the better you're doing; however, for some questions the opposite is true. We learned from experience that adding these reversed types of questions (which we've marked with an asterisk) slows people down and gives them time to reflect before grading themselves, making their scores more realistic.

Note that because of this varied rating scale, you cannot easily add up your numbers for a total or average NewSmart Behaviors score. We did that because an average or total score could mask significant sub-behavior weaknesses. Our message is that you have to excel at many sub-behaviors in order to excel at the big behavior. An average or total score won't help you do that. Ed has used this diagnostic with several hundred people in his teaching and consulting. We're sharing it here because many of those people found it helpful in assessing their weaknesses and in creating a NewSmart Behaviors Personal Improvement Plan.

Please note that this is only a tool—it has not been statistically validated. The tool's purpose is to provide you with information, and it'll be useful to you only if you're totally honest about assessing yourself. To get a realistic picture, some people have found it helpful to have other trusted people also assess them. Ed has also learned from experience that many people decide to retake the diagnostic after the first attempt because they realize that they weren't brutally honest with themselves the first time through. How do you know if you're being brutally honest? See if you gave yourself a lot of 4s and 5s the first time around (and 1s and 2s for the questions with an asterisk). Were those scores really justified?

Following the assessment are some instructions for reflecting on your results. You're asked to state what you've learned. You may find that you have lots of areas that need improvement. Most people do because few of us have ever had any formal training on these behaviors. That's right: few of us have had formal training on how to excel at the key NewSmart Behaviors, so don't get discouraged if you need to improve on all of them. We have also learned that many of those who have had some training on a particular behavior don't necessarily practice the behaviors as much as they think. There's often a big gap between what we know and what we actually do.

## 1. Quieting Ego

*1 = Never  2 = Very Rarely  3 = Infrequently  4 = Sometimes  5 = Regularly*

I actively try every day to quiet my ego.

I'm aware when I'm becoming very "me" oriented.

I evaluate my level of Humility daily and whether I was arrogant or "all about me."

I believe that "I'm not my ideas."

I understand that "it's not all about me."

I like telling people about my accomplishments.*

I like being the center of attention.*

I tend to dominate conversations.*

I have been told that I'm arrogant.*

Work colleagues would say that I know my weaknesses.

I often say: "I don't know."

When I act badly at work, I apologize to that person (in public if the act occurred in public).

I take ownership publicly of my mistakes.

I'm open about my weaknesses and ask people at work for help.

I believe that I'm special and better than many people.*

I react defensively when someone disagrees with me.*

I think a lot about whether people think I'm smart.*

I think a lot about how I'm perceived.*

I avoid situations where I may not look good.*

In a conversation, I want the other person to leave thinking I'm smart.*

I frequently put myself emotionally into another person's shoes.

I believe that leaders must be strong and not show weakness.*

I thank others often.

I'm sensitive to when I'm getting defensive.

I must leave each engagement winning.*

I use mindfulness to quiet my ego.

I'm compassionate with others.

I accept that I'm a suboptimal thinker and listener.

I seek praise.*

I seek negative feedback.

## 2(a). Managing Self (Thinking)

*1 = Never  2 = Very Rarely  3 = Infrequently  4 = Sometimes  5 = Regularly*

I'm open-minded.

I'm fair-minded.

I'm mindful—really present in the moment with my full attention.

Frequently during the day I slow myself down to think deeply.

I use data to make my decisions.

I'm very curious.

I'm good at not knowing—I frequently say "I don't know."

*What* is right is more important to me than *who* is right.

I'm paranoid about missing something and about being overconfident.

I confront the brutal facts—even if they make me look bad.

I approach having difficult conversations; I don't avoid them.

I exhibit intellectual humility in my interactions with everyone.

I have learned to decouple my ego from my beliefs.

I actively manage my thinking daily.

I'm aware of when I need to slow down to think.

I use good thinking processes daily.

I use good collaborating processes daily.

I grade myself daily and keep a learning journal.

I have a checklist of my "needs to improve."

I share my "needs to improve" with teammates and ask them to help me improve.

I role-model humility, including intellectual humility.

I role-model learning resiliency—bouncing back quickly from mistakes and failures.

I critique ideas, not people.

I give all my associates the permission to speak freely.

I reward candor.

I'm honest and transparent about my weaknesses and mistakes.

I actively seek constructive feedback about my thinking from others.

I unpack the assumptions underlying my thoughts daily.

I seek to stress-test some of my thoughts or beliefs daily.

I evaluate the results of my decisions and lessons learned.

I worry about my biases.

I have devised ways to mitigate my biases.

I use mental rehearsal daily to play things out in my mind.

I use mental replay daily to reflect on my actions and decisions in order to learn.

At least two times a week, I tell a peer or employee: "I don't know."

At least two times a week, I ask a peer or employee to critique my thinking.

I ask my direct reports monthly to give me candid feedback on my performance.

I tell myself daily that I have to think deeper about an issue.

## 2(b). Managing Self (Emotions)

*1 = Never  2 = Very Rarely  3 = Infrequently  4 = Sometimes  5 = Regularly*

I'm very sensitive to my emotions.

I label my emotions.

I try to understand why I'm feeling what I feel.

I actively choose whether to engage with an emotion or let it pass.

I know when I'm feeling defensive or fearful.

I actively manage my fears.

I understand what makes me feel fearful.

I frequently take deep breaths to calm myself.

I frequently think about something positive in my life to reduce my fear.

I'm sensitive to my body language.

I'm sensitive to how others are receiving my message.

I'm sensitive to others' emotions.

I'm sensitive to others' body language and tone.

I take others' emotions into account when conversing.

I try to approach meetings and others with a positive emotional state.

I use deep breaths to manage my emotions.

I try to put myself in a positive emotional state before thinking deeply about something.

I actively try to manage my emotions.

I know how to and frequently prevent my emotions from hijacking my thinking.

## 3. Reflective Listening

*1 = Never  2 = Very Rarely  3 = Infrequently  4 = Sometimes  5 = Regularly*

I'm a nonjudgmental listener.

I'm a nondefensive listener.

When I listen, I focus on whether the speaker agrees with me.*

I often get bored listening to others, so my mind wanders.*

I interrupt people when I know the answer.*

I often paraphrase and repeat back what I think the speaker is saying, and ask if I'm hearing him or her correctly.

If I don't understand, I often ask the speaker to say it a different way.

I apologize when I interrupt someone speaking to me.

I begin formulating my answer/response in my head while someone is talking.*

While listening, I'm aware of my body reactions.

I finish people's sentences out loud or in my head.*

As I listen, I try to make eye contact with the speaker.

As I listen, I'm aware of my emotions.

Before engaging in an important conversation, I ask myself if I'm ready to be open-minded.

Before engaging in an important conversation, I calm my emotions.

I usually don't answer quickly; I reflect.

While listening, I'm sensitive to the speaker's emotions, tone, and body language.

In difficult conversations, before responding, I thank the speaker for having the courage to talk.

I often assume that I know what the speaker will say next.*

I often ask questions intended to confirm my view.*

I often ask questions that will lead the speaker toward my view.*

When listening, I pause to "try on" the person's ideas or beliefs to see how it feels.

I listen to learn, not to confirm.

I multitask when I listen.*

I multitask when I talk on the phone.*

I multitask when I attend meetings virtually.*


## 4. Otherness (Emotionally Connecting and Relating)

*1 = Never  2 = Very Rarely  3 = Infrequently  4 = Sometimes  5 = Regularly*

I know my EI weaknesses and have a plan to improve them.

I relate personally to people before getting to business.

I try to demonstrate to people that I care about them.

I try to understand where people are coming from.

I try to be an emotionally positive person.

I try to be totally honest with people.

I evaluate the quality of my emotional connections daily.

I'm sensitive to the messages I send through my body language.

I stop and make sure before I enter each meeting that I'm emotionally and mentally prepared to be present—to be fully attentive in that meeting.

I view collaboration as a competition to see who is right.*

My goal in collaborating is to avoid looking dumb.*

Another goal in collaboration is to not "lose face."*

I stop regularly to engage with people during the day.

I do "check-ins" with my direct reports and ask about them as people.

I ask people at the end of a meeting whether they're in a "good place."

In collaborating, I try to inquire as much as I advocate.

In collaborating, I act as if *what* is accurate is more important than *who* is right.

In collaborating, I focus on *what* is wrong, not *who* is wrong.

In collaborating, I'm mindful of who is not engaged.

In collaborating, I seek to engage the quiet ones.

In collaborating, I'm mindful of the "elephant in the room."

In collaborating, I often will raise the hard issue or talk about the "elephant."

In collaborating, if I don't know, I say so.

In collaborating, I'm mindful of my body reactions and body language.

I'm aware when I react defensively.

I usually tell people what to do or how to do it.*

I go out of my way to show gratitude to people.

Every day I ask people with whom I work how they're doing, and I show them that I care about their answers.

I smile at people.

I slow down and connect—even for a short time.

I'm direct, courteous, and honest with others.

I keep my word and my commitments.

I'm authentic with others.

I engender trust by taking the first step to be vulnerable.

I focus on others when conversing with them.

I truly try to get to know others deeply so I can understand them.

I don't gossip about others.

I keep in confidence things said to me in confidence.

I keep in confidence things said to me by others when they're being courageously vulnerable.

I thank people for having the courage to challenge my ideas.

## What Did I Learn from My Diagnostic?

Now you're ready to review and make meaning of your results. Go slowly, line by line (that is, sub-behavior by sub-behavior). Focus on those statements for which you gave yourself a low grade. What do your results "say" to you? What are the sub-behaviors that you need to work on? We recommend that you make a list of those sub-behaviors.

Now what?

### Step 1: Prioritize the behaviors and sub-behaviors

We suggest starting with the NewSmart Behavior that's the lowest on the NewSmart Behavior pyramid shown below. Although the behaviors overlap in many ways and reinforce each other, we find that it's easier for many people to think about them building on each other from the bottom up. For example, if you scored poorly on Quieting Ego and Reflective Listening, start with Quieting Ego. Then, look at your list of underlying sub-behaviors that need improving. Pick one or two sub-behaviors on which you scored poorly.

NewSmart + Humility

## Step 2: Talk it out

After picking your sub-behaviors, have conversations with other people you trust about the behaviors you want to improve and why you want to improve them. Ask people to be on the watch for how you're doing and ask them to give you feedback. Ask for their support and encouragement. Talking about why you want to change a behavior helps you "make meaning" of the information and can create more of a commitment to change. If you're seeking to curb a bad behavior, try to figure out why you're behaving that way and how you are benefiting from the bad behavior. Talk about this with a trusted other. We have found that figuring out the "why" is also much easier if you talk it out with someone.

## Step 3: Learn the science of improving

One purpose of this book is to invite you to take your thinking, listening, relating, and collaborating skills to a much higher level in order to excel and even become an expert. Some of the best work and research on achieving high mental performance comes from Lyle Bourne and Alice Healy of the University of Colorado in *Train Your Mind for Peak Performance* and from Anders Ericsson of Florida State University in *PEAK: Secrets from the New Science of Expertise*. The work of these experts emphasizes the importance of having the discipline to practice daily; the importance of real-time feedback; and the importance of "deliberate" practice, which is practice focused on improving in a certain way specific behaviors or parts of behaviors that underlie a skill.

What does this mean for you in this context? To become expert at NewSmart Behaviors requires self-discipline, high motivation, perseverance, and practice, practice, practice.

Training and deliberate practice are specific to the particular skill. For example, not interrupting is a necessary sub-behavior of Reflective Listening, but alone it's not sufficient to excel at this crucial NewSmart Behavior. To excel may require improvement in many other sub-behaviors of Reflective Listening.

*How* you practice is also important—the key is to do it deliberately by breaking down the desired behavior into its component parts. That's why we focus on sub-behaviors. Let's assume, for example, that many of you, like almost all the several hundred people to whom Ed has given the NewSmart Behaviors Assessment over the past few years, determined that you need to improve your Reflective Listening. Unfortunately, you can't just start practicing Reflective Listening. Instead, you need to isolate specific parts of Reflective Listening that you want to improve. The tools and content in chapters 4–7 can be helpful in delineating those component parts.

Let's assume that you determined you need to be mindfully present and open-minded when you enter a conversation and that you need to stop interrupting people and ask questions to make sure you understand what the other person just said before advocating or telling her or him your view. Think about those three component behaviors logically. Which makes sense to work on first? It would seem to us that you have to be mindfully present and open-minded to do the other two behaviors.

### Step 4: Get advice from an "expert"
Do you know individuals who are good at Reflective Listening? Are you comfortable seeking advice from them? Tell them that you respect the way they listen to others and that you're trying

to be a better listener. Ask them how they stay focused and, for example, how they refrain from formulating their answers while other people are talking. Ask them how they learned to ask questions before responding. How do they self-monitor themselves? What advice do they have about "how to" be mindfully present and open-minded?

### Step 5: Create your experiment

Let's assume that to improve your Reflective Listening you've decided to work first on being mindfully present to listen with an open mind. How do you do that? You may want to refer to chapter 6 for some ideas. Assume that you decide to use the premeeting guide from chapter 6 that prepares you to be mindful and emotionally positive. OK, so, your first experiment is to prepare before each conversation to be mindfully present and to stay focused on the speaker and his or her words, listening to understand what he or she is saying before thinking about your response.

### Step 6: "Warm up"

Continuing with the example in step 5, you could do the following: before each conversation, take four deep breaths, counting to four on the inhale and again on the exhale. Think of something or someone who evokes strong positive feelings for you—maybe a loved one, your pet, a dear friend, or someone who did a nice thing for you. Then repeat these sentences: "I am not my ideas," "My mental models are not reality," "This is not all about me," and "Listen to learn, not to confirm."

Now mentally visualize how you'll behave and how it'll feel. Think about how you'll sit. What posture relaxes you? Think about the position of your hands—open or closed?

Think about smiling often. Think about maintaining eye contact with the speaker. See yourself sitting calmly in the meeting really focused with all your being on listening. See yourself bringing your attention back to the present if your mind wanders or if you begin to formulate your response while the person is talking. Rehearse in your mind what you'll do if you begin to lose your focus in the meeting. For example, perhaps you'll tell yourself "come back to listening" or "let that thought pass or float on by."

## Step 7: Deliberately practice

Now engage in those behaviors every opportunity you have today and tomorrow and the next day, and the next. Remember that knowing what to do is not the same as doing it consistently and excellently. Building new habits requires motivation, focus, and repetition.

## Step 8: Measure yourself

Continuing with our experiment, now is the time to measure your progress. At the end of the particular conversation, take a few minutes and mentally replay it in your head and grade yourself. How many times did you daydream? How many times did you create your response in your head while the other person was talking? How many times did you think about some other matter? How many times did you recognize that you were losing focus and bring back your attention? Keep a record. Write down your self-feedback. What steps did you do well? Record your results and track your results daily and monthly.

Soon thereafter, think about the times you were not mindfully present. What were you doing instead? Is there a pattern?

Try to recall how you felt then. Were you bored? Worried about your next meeting? Feeling defensive? Feeling what? Trying to understand when you lose focus or why may help create an early warning system that alerts you when to work even harder on focusing.

Grade yourself in every meeting for a few days and talk frequently with your trusted others who are monitoring your progress. Perhaps you're making progress on a few items, but not making as much progress on, say, not formulating your response while the speaker is still talking. You could then focus more on mentally rehearsing and preparing yourself before each meeting to "listen to understand" and ask questions to make sure that you understand what the person is saying before you respond. Feel good about the progress you make. It will come at different speeds for different sub-behaviors. But stay disciplined. It could really help to get feedback from trusted others who observe you in the meetings. Many of us go mindlessly from meeting to meeting. Plan for a five-minute break between meetings for reflection and grading or at least reflect while you walk to the next meeting.

If your plan isn't working, go back to the expert and seek advice. Ask other excellent listeners how they do the specific behavior. Don't give up. Try something new and keep working at it until you make progress. Remember, we're not talking about creating an Einstein formula, we're talking about managing how you listen. You may have to try several different approaches—the key is to keep working at it. What have we found in our work with others? Too many people lack the self-discipline to work at this. And those who do work hard see positive results at work and in their personal lives, which further motivates them to keep working.

## Step 9: Be patient, savor small improvements, and persevere

One lesson we have learned from our research is that people who are very good at thinking, listening, relating, and managing their thinking and emotions never take it for granted. They stay focused on it daily by using processes, checklists, templates, and feedback. They are constructively paranoid about slippage and reverting to our natural proclivities of lazy thinking and emotional defensiveness. They understand that it requires motivation to excel and self-discipline to work daily on improving themselves.

You will make mistakes. Learn from them and stay the course. Take it one day at a time. You'll never reach perfection, but you can incrementally improve. You'll be trying to reverse decades of habits. It won't happen quickly, but progress can be made. Striving to reach your highest potential is a never-ending process that can be a meaningful learning journey in itself.

I (Ed) will give you an example of my long and winding journey to improve my Reflective Listening abilities. As I've said, I realized that I wasn't a good listener because I often interrupted people in conversations and meetings. I wanted to stop that behavior, so I decided that I'd wait until a person stopped talking and then count to ten before I spoke. That didn't work. Then I decided that I would put the heel of my right foot on the instep of my left foot and press down hard if I started to interrupt someone. That also didn't work, but it did hurt a lot.

I realized that I needed some additional help and reached out to a close friend who happened to be the colleague of Robert Kegan and Lisa Laskow Lahey, the authors of *Immunity to Change*. In their book Kegan and Lahey explained that most people behave the way they do because it produces some favorable result. As such, it's hard to change those behaviors unless you unpack the reasons why you behave that way and then deal with the underlying belief.[1]

In two hourlong telephone calls with my friend, I finally got to the nub: I interrupted people because I believed it resulted in looking smart (not arrogant, inconsiderate, and rude). Deep down I believed that if I didn't get the right answer before someone else spoke, then other people wouldn't think I was that competent. That was my big assumption. To change that behavior, then, I had to run an experiment—if I didn't interrupt people and they still thought that I was competent, then my assumption would be proved false and I could more easily change this behavior.

So I committed to not interrupting people in meetings and then sought feedback on my new behavior. Turned out that no one thought I wasn't competent simply because I listened and tried to understand others before advocating my position. In fact, some people said that they thought the new behavior made me more effective in meetings and that they liked the fact that I had stopped being a rude person who interrupted. I share this story because it demonstrates that changing behaviors can be hard and may require unpacking the reasons that you behave the way you do and changing your mental model about that behavior.

# Part 3

# The NewSmart Organization

# 9

# Leading a NewSmart
# Organization

In this chapter we turn our focus to the organization of the future and to creating the kind of work environment most conducive to humans excelling at the four SMA Skills and reaching their highest potential in the SMA. To do that requires an organizational system in which the structure, culture, human resource policies, leadership behaviors, measurements, rewards, and processes are aligned seamlessly in a self-reinforcing manner that embraces and encourages the NewSmart + Humility mental model and NewSmart Behaviors. We don't know what the future will be like. However, based on our work, we believe that the following is more likely than not:

1. The organization of the future will likely look a lot different than the organization of today because of converging forces of change: technology, demographic shifts, the loci of economic growth in the world, and ever-increasing transparency, connectivity, change, and uncertainty.

2. In most cases, the organization of the future will likely be staffed by some combination of smart robots, smart thinking

machines, and humans, with humans doing those tasks that complement technology or that technology can't do well.

3. Technology will likely play a major role in the following business functions: accounting, quality controls, finance, operations, marketing, strategy, logistics, distribution, and decision analysis. That will likely mean a reduction in the number of human employees, and in some industries that reduction could be quite large.

4. Operational excellence will likely be technology-driven and thus commoditized, leaving innovation as the primary value creator and differentiator for many businesses.

5. For most organizations, the only sustainable competitive advantage long-term will likely be the ability to learn and adapt faster than the competition.

6. In that case, human development will likely become an individual and organizational strategic imperative, because humans will need to excel at continuous learning, and we believe that requires excelling at the NewSmart Behaviors.

7. Talented humans will be in high demand globally and will likely place higher value on the meaningfulness of work and on their own growth and development than on the location of work or their longevity of employment with any one employer.

8. Humans will be needed to do the four SMA Skills: higher-order critical thinking, innovative thinking, creativity, and high emotional engagement with other people. Leaders and managers will be needed to create the right conditions that enable the highest levels of human performance and orchestrate the

connectivity and integration of technology and humans in order to create value in constantly evolving environments.

9. Humans will likely have to be more agile and adaptive, updating their mental models based on changing realities, and organizations will have to update their value propositions. Organizations and their human talent must excel at iterative learning, dealing with complexity, and creating value through innovation.

10. An organization's competitive advantage from a human perspective likely will depend on how well its humans over-come their natural proclivities to be confirmation-biased, emotionally defensive thinkers whose thinking and abilities to effectively work in teams are suboptimized by ego and fears. That could mean that the most successful companies in some industries will be those that excel at human development in addition to their core business.

11. Every organization will likely confront three big existential questions:

> Will the organization be able to learn, adapt, and innovate to meet stakeholder needs faster than its competition?

> Will the organization be able to create an environment that enables and promotes the highest levels of human develop-ment, human engagement, and human excellence in criti-cal thinking, creativity, and innovation?

> Will the organization be able to attract, develop, and retain the best human learners, thinkers, and collaborators?

How does an organization redesign itself to meet these challenges? First, we believe it requires putting the right people in the right environment using the right kinds of processes. Such a system should enable and drive NewSmart Behaviors. An innovative organization must have innovators. An industry-disrupting organization must have disruptors. A learning organization must have learners. At least for the near future, that means humans who excel at the SMA Skills and, thus, the NewSmart Behaviors.

Second, we believe that the answer will not be found in economics, finance, strategy, engineering, or computer science. We believe that the answer will be found in the science of learning and in cognitive, social, positive, educational, and clinical psychology. We believe that the cultural and leadership model for the organization of the future will be based on three psychological concepts:

1. Positivity
2. Self-Determination Theory
3. Psychological Safety

We explain what we mean by those concepts and show how they create an environment that will help humans embrace NewSmart and overcome ego and fear. As the renowned Humanistic psychologist Abraham Maslow states, a person "reaches out to the environment in wonder and interest, and expresses whatever skills he has, to the extent that he is not crippled by fear, to the extent that he feels safe enough to dare."[1]

## Technology Will Humanize Business

This new type of work environment that enables the highest levels of human thinking and emotional engagement is quite different from the environments that exist in many organizations today, which in most cases are based on Old Smart and outdated Industrial Age management philosophies and processes. We believe that the organization of the future will need to be a people-centric, hyperlearning organization that fuses the best technologies and the best human learners to excel at innovating to meet the needs of its stakeholders.

To be a "best human learner" will require much more than technical skills. It will require high-level cognitive and emotional skills, too. Humans will need to excel at "being good at not knowing"; thinking like a scientist; mitigating fear and ego; Reflective Listening; "making meaning" collaboration; emotionally connecting and relating to other people; operating in environments characterized by uncertainty, ambiguity, and complexity; and continually updating their mental models to better reflect reality.

Humans will have to evolve and develop their thinking and emotional skills to a level much higher than most of us are used to. To attract, develop, and retain the best human learners—the best human talent—an organization must be designed using the science of adult learning to create the type of environment that enables and promotes the desired optimizing mindsets and behaviors and negates the mindsets and behaviors that will suboptimize performance. While technology will dehumanize businesses by reducing the number of employees, ironically, it will also require businesses to become more humanized with respect to the human employees who remain.

Let's again compare the "old way" with the potentially humanizing "new way."

| Old Cultural Ways | New Cultural Ways |
| --- | --- |
| Individuals win | Teams win |
| Play cards close to the chest | Transparency |
| Highest-ranking person can trump | Best idea or argument wins |
| Listening to confirm | Listening to learn |
| Telling | Asking questions |
| Knowing | Being good at not knowing |
| IQ | IQ & EQ |
| Mistakes are always bad | Mistakes are learning opportunities |
| Compete | Collaborate |
| Self-promote | Self-reflect |

Some organizations are already on this journey to the "new way." They include science- and technology-based businesses such as Google and Intuit; creativity-based businesses like Pixar and IDEO; investment managers like Bridgewater Associates; and the US military Special Operations Forces, such as the Navy SEALs.

Recall from chapters 2 and 3 how in their own ways those organizations embrace NewSmart and the Humility mindset in their cultures and leadership behaviors. All those organizations operate on a model of "hiring" for cultural fit and recruit people who are most likely to flourish in a team environment characterized by high-energy hyperlearning. They understand that putting the right people in the right culture using the right learning processes will produce the highest levels of human performance.

### It's All about Emotions

Hyperlearning is learning that's agile, rapid, energizing, engaged, determined, continual, and eager. For humans, that learning is both cognitive and emotional. Most businesses have analytical thinking processes and innovation thinking processes. That's necessary for hyperlearning, but it's not sufficient. What hasn't been emphasized enough in most organizations are the emotionally challenging parts of effective learning—the emotional parts of critical thinking, creativity, innovation, collaborating, and engaging with others. In the SMA, optimal human performance will require high emotional competencies, including emotional intelligence and the abilities to manage our ego and fears and emotionally connect and relate with others.

A few years ago Ed facilitated a conversation among seven heads of innovation and research and development from several innovative, well-known public companies. He asked them individually to compile answers to the following questions:

1. What are the biggest individual inhibitors of innovation?
2. What are the key attributes of an innovator?
3. What are the key things that a company can do to accelerate innovation?

The number one answers to each question were, respectively, fear, fearlessness or intellectual courage, and having the CEO own and role-model innovation behaviors through her or his thinking, listening, and relating. What kind of work environment enables those results? Over thirty years of research in psychology, organizational behavior, and leadership strongly suggests the answer: people are more likely to consistently excel if they work in an environment that cultivates Positivity, meets their innate needs for Self-Determination, and gives them Psychological Safety.

## The Power of Positive Emotions

Leading research by cognitive, social, and positive psychologists including Barbara Fredrickson and Alice Isen has produced strong evidence that positive emotions enable and enhance cognitive processing, innovative thinking, and creativity and lead to better judgments and decision making. On the flip side, research has shown that negative emotions—especially fear and anxiety—have the opposite effect. Fears and anxiety in the workplace can take many forms, including fears of looking bad, speaking up, making mistakes, losing your job, or not being liked.

All of us are insecure and fearful to a certain extent and in certain situations. The differences are just a matter of degree and how we handle them. We want to be liked. We want to be accepted by the team. We want to fit in. Even if we practice Quieting Ego and Managing Self (thinking and emotions), we won't be able to think, learn, or collaborate with others at our best if the work environment is emotionally negative.

**The work environment must be designed to reduce fears, insecurities, and other negative emotions. That means the environment needs to be humanistic.** This concurs with eight major research studies that found that consistent high-performance businesses have high employee engagement, and that occurs in people-centric cultures.[2] In this type of culture, leadership behaviors, HR policies, measurements, and rewards all send a consistent and self-reinforcing message: people are highly valued and cared about in the organization. These organizations have high mutual accountability. They are not "easy" places to work because the standards are high, but the environment is positive. Additional organizations that Ed has researched that meet this standard include Sysco, United Parcel Service, Trilogy Health Services, Southwest Airlines, Starbucks, W. L. Gore & Associates, US Marine Corps, and Levy Restaurants.

---

### Reflection Time

Think about the jobs you've had where you were able to perform at your highest levels. What kind of environment existed?

How did you feel in those environments?

Think about the jobs that you felt were just a way to earn a living. What were those environments like?

How did you feel in those environments?

In which environment did you do your best work?

---

Having worked in emotionally positive and emotionally negative environments, we, unsurprisingly, have found positive environments to be more energizing, caring, inspiring, fun, and meaningful, and we worked harder with less energy expenditure because those environments were psychologically uplifting. Positivity contributed to our motivation, helping us do our best work. It wasn't easy. Standards were very high, but because the environments valued people, we felt appreciated, and we, in turn, valued and appreciated our teammates. We looked forward to work and we were happier, so we were learning, thinking, and collaborating better. Those positive effects went home with us. Our children and spouses noticed our positive dispositions. We were nicer to be around.

## Our Needs for Self-Determination

Self-Determination Theory (SDT), initially developed by the psychologists Edward L. Deci and Richard Ryan, is one of the most well-known theories of human motivation. According to SDT, intrinsic motivation—the tendency to seek out new and challenging situations and expand cognitive and behavioral capacities for their own sake as opposed to fulfilling social obligations or gaining some extrinsic reward—is supported when three innate human needs are met:

1. Autonomy: experiencing a feeling of volition and initiative.
2. Relatedness: establishing a sense of mutual respect and reliance with others.
3. Competence: succeeding at optimally challenging tasks and being able to attain desired outcomes.[3]

As Ed details in *Learn or Die: Using Science to Build a Leading-Edge Learning Organization*, three decades of research on high-performance businesses show that high employee engagement is correlated with high performance, and decades of research on what creates high employee engagement tell us that the key factors all relate to meeting an individual's needs for Self-Determination. If employees feel that they have autonomy, relatedness, and effectiveness at work, then they're more likely to be highly engaged and thus more likely to perform at high levels.

## Autonomy

What does it mean to create an environment that satisfies the innate human need for autonomy? It doesn't mean simply providing independence. Nor is it merely a lack of micromanagement or giving people a superficial sense of control over their daily tasks. It requires giving people the opportunity for input and choice and engaging them in making meaning as to why what they're doing is important for the organization's success and in line with their values. It means providing people a feeling of being respected, held in positive regard, and listened to. It's not treating people as cogs in a wheel. What this really comes down to is a caring interpersonal relationship with one's supervisor or manager.

A recent company-wide research project at Facebook showed the importance of this. In 2016 Facebook disclosed the findings of a study of its highest-performing teams. The purpose was to learn what the managers did to get that high performance. The number one finding was that high-performance managers at Facebook cared about their team members.[4] Likewise, decades of research by Gallup, Inc. on its Q12 Employee Engagement diagnostic have shown that the most important factor in job satisfaction is how your boss treats you. Those findings are all about autonomy—being respected as an individual—and that involves being held in positive regard as a unique human being by others and most importantly by your boss.

Having posed those questions to thousands of business managers and leaders over the last decade, we would guess that your answers were determined largely by whether your boss treated you in ways that met your need for autonomy, which resulted in you feeling respected as a person. Just as with Positivity, how people *feel* counts. How people feel depends on how they're treated and how they see other people being treated. That depends primarily on a company's culture and processes and the behaviors of managers and leaders. Good intentions are not enough. Value and mission statements are not behaviors. If you're a leader or manager, behaviors count—even small behaviors.

---

### Reflection Time

Have you ever worked at a place where you felt respected as a person as opposed to feeling like you were only a cog in someone else's money-making machine? What did that feel like?

Have you ever worked at a place where your boss took the time to get to know you as a person? Where he or she sought out your opinion on things pertaining to your job? How did that feel?

Who was the best boss you ever had? Why was she or he the best? What did your boss do to make you feel that way?

Now think about the worst manager or boss you ever had. Why was she or he so bad? What did your boss do to make you feel this? How did you feel about working for that person?

---

## Relatedness

The second part of SDT—relatedness—is provided through meaningful close personal relationships at work. We believe that this requires an organization to create the opportunities for people to connect and build trust with others. It means allocating time and designing work environments that bring people together to relate about nonwork matters. It means small teams taking time to talk about how each person is doing personally. It means that NewSmart managers and leaders understand that building trust is an investment of time, but that once built, trust pays off through more effective collaboration, thinking, creating, and innovating.

## Competence

The third innate psychological need according to SDT is to be effective in and master our environment. That requires a manager or leader to take the time to really get to know employees as people—their strengths, weaknesses, and goals—as well as to help them get the right training or opportunities to develop and provide feedback. It requires managers to be held accountable for their people's development.

In sum, engaging individuals in the courageous pursuit of continuous learning and innovation requires that they be highly engaged both cognitively and emotionally in their work. The science demonstrates that high engagement is more likely to happen if the work environment is a people-centric, emotionally positive one in which an individual's Self-Determination needs are met through the actions of leaders, managers, and teammates.

---

### Reflection Time

So far we have discussed the need for the work environment to be emotionally positive and meet Self-Determination needs. Does it make sense to you why those psychological concepts will enable the highest levels of human thinking and engagement?

Do you agree that people need to feel valued and safe in order to be able to expend their maximum energy on being focused outward as opposed to being focused inward on protecting their egos?

Do you agree that if people feel devalued and fearful, they won't be able to perform at their best?

---

## Psychological Safety

Mitigating fear in the workplace also requires Psychological Safety. Studies show that without Psychological Safety, people will not fully embrace the hard parts of thinking and innovating: the giving and receiving of constructive feedback; challenging the status quo; asking and being asked the hard questions; being nondefensive, open-minded, and intellectually courageous; and having the courage to try new things and fail. Amy Edmondson, a professor at the Harvard Business School, has conducted some of the best research on Psychological Safety and found that it's an essential element of organizational learning.

Feeling psychologically safe is feeling safe from retribution, which could be social ostracism, being passed over for good assignments, having bonuses or raises reduced, or even being transferred out of the team or fired on trumped-up charges. As Adam Grant, a Wharton professor, states in his latest book, *Originals: How Non-Conformists Move the World*, "Most of us opt to fit in rather than stand out."[5] That's especially true in organizations that have cultures of fear or leaders who are autocratic, command-and-control types or arrogant, all-knowing types. **Psychologically safe environments have cultures of candor, permission to speak freely, and permission to make learning mistakes (within financial risk parameters), and they offer all employees a voice by devaluing elitism, hierarchy, and rank (other than with respect to compensation).**

Feeling psychologically safe enables people to (1) seek constructive feedback and challenges to their thinking and (2) feel safe giving feedback and challenging others' thinking, including higher-ups in the organization. Feeling safe enables speaking up, having the courage to try new things, and behaving in ways that reflect NewSmart. Feeling safe is required for curiosity and having the courage to explore and innovate. Feeling safe means that you feel that your boss, your employer, and your colleagues will do you no harm as you try to learn.

But speaking up in front of higher-ups goes against our upbringing of respecting hierarchy and deferring to our parents and elders. And many people are afraid to speak up or stand out from the crowd. Psychologically safe environments have to mitigate all those inhibitors and enable and reward speaking-up behaviors. We aren't talking about arrogant "telling" when we refer to speaking up. We're talking about the types of collaboration based on asking questions to find the best answers.

It's not enough to give permission to speak freely. Speaking freely should be acknowledged and emotionally rewarded publicly. Leadership and manager behaviors that negate Psychological Safety should not be tolerated. Leaders and managers must embrace NewSmart and the Humility mindset and role-model NewSmart Behaviors, including Quieting Ego and Reflective Listening, and publicly seek challenges to their views and beliefs. In this type of environment, leaders have to

---

### Reflection Time

Have you ever worked in an organization or with or for a person with whom you didn't feel psychologically safe? At a place where you didn't have permission to speak freely or where making mistakes was punished?

What did that feel like?

Could you be your best self?

---

be human, too. Overbearing, all-knowing, elitist leaders will be severely challenged in this new world.

I (Ed) have been very fortunate. I have worked in only one organization in my career that was not a psychologically safe environment—a place where I felt at risk if I raised difficult issues or disagreed with the group. I avoided meetings with the CEO because he made it clear that he wanted to hear only good news. It was a downer. I had to be so careful. I couldn't be my best self under that CEO. I was disappointed in myself if I kept quiet, but I also was disappointed when I spoke up and was punished for it, which happened. I was on guard and tense at work because I had to monitor what I said and to whom. I didn't trust the system. People were not held accountable for bad performance or bad behaviors because the culture instead punished difficult conversations. As a result, I focused entirely on my work and my team and spent as little time as possible in meetings with higher-ups. When I had to attend those meetings, I learned to just keep quiet.

To this day, I'm disappointed in myself for not speaking up more. In my decades of work, it was the only time I was a coward. My friends tell me that I was a "smart" coward because it would have been more harmful to me and my family if I had spoken up and lost my job. It made me more committed to never making anyone who worked with me or for me feel that way. Since then, when people have the courage to speak up, I publicly thank them for having that courage, and I try hard to receive feedback in a respectful, nondefensive way. Thankfully, that CEO's tenure was short.

## The Power of Caring and Trust

Does human thriving and flourishing economically in the SMA really come down to our feelings? Yes, in many cases it's all about how we feel at work and how our work environment makes us feel. Organizations that want to attract and retain the best talent and make the most of their human talent in the SMA will design their entire internal management systems to drive leader and management behaviors that promote Positivity, meet Self-Determination needs, provide Psychological Safety, and result in caring about people as individuals. Google and Pixar get this "feeling stuff." They try to create safe and trusting environments through their culture, processes, measurements, and rewards, and through leaders and managers who role-model NewSmart Behaviors. Their organizational systems are designed to mitigate ego, fear, and mistrust. Like most things in business, the principles are simple: it's the daily, disciplined execution that's hard.

When we talk about feelings with some leaders, we get the following reaction: "Well, if we care about people, they will take advantage of us and standards will get lower. We can't be perceived as 'soft.'" Here's our response: The research clearly shows that caring about people and holding high standards are not mutually exclusive. A friend of Ed's who led a very successful innovation transformation at a consumer products company explained the purpose of a caring environment this way: "We had to make it safe for our people to not just sit, stay, and heel." What that means is command-and-control, autocratic leadership models will not work in organizations that need people to be agile, adaptive hyperlearners. It also means that many human resource functions will have to be completely transformed into human development teams to help people

169

develop their cognitive and emotional skills so they can excel at doing what technology can't do well.

We know that innovation happens best when diverse people work in small project teams. That will in and of itself make emotional intelligence and relational "soft" skills highly valued human capabilities. That will be a new emphasis for many people. Recall the research involving the effectiveness of small teams in solving problems or creating new ideas, which found that the higher the proportion of women on a team, the better the results. Women tend to score higher than men on emotional intelligence and lower than men on narcissism.[6] As a result, we may well see even more women in senior executive positions in the SMA.

**This means one thing: a NewSmart organization, irrespective of what it does or sells, will be a human development organization in the business of learning.** Human development is just that—an individual human development plan for every employee and every employee having a manager responsible for helping her or him develop. Because the organization of the future will in many cases have far fewer human employees than it does today, scaling that individual development process becomes easier. It may require small team structures that cascade up into larger groups. Managers would have responsibility for helping their teams of seven to ten people develop their skills to the highest level possible—a requirement for adding value to that organization in the SMA.

Time now to look closer at Google and Pixar, which are already well on their way to being NewSmart organizations of the future. We've already introduced ways in which their cultures and leaders embrace NewSmart and Humility. Now we'll explore how they cultivate Positivity in their work environments, meet their employees' needs for Self-Determination, and provide Psychological Safety.

### Google's Innovative Hyperlearning Environment

Google (Alphabet, Inc.) was founded in 1998 and in its fiscal year ending December 31, 2015, had about $75 billion in revenue with margins in excess of 20 percent. Its market value was nearly $500 billion. Google is a technology-based company with over fifty thousand employees and well known as being highly innovative. Examples are its current work with driverless cars; Google glass, contact lenses that monitor glucose levels; balloons that provide Internet connectivity; and artificial intelligence like AlphaGo. When many people think of Google as an employer, they think of great perks and a playful work environment, but what we also discovered through our research is that Google has intentionally designed an innovation system to enable the highest levels of human performance.

It's no secret that Google's culture emanates from its founders, who have been vocal about wanting to create a company where work is meaningful and people and their families feel cared for. As evidenced by the values of the founders and the processes they've incorporated, they believe that people do their most creative and innovative work in environments that provide trust, the right tools, and plenty of opportunities. Google is interesting because it seeks to hire what it calls "smart creatives"—people who are independent thinkers. Google has a list of attributes that it looks for in new hires, and one of the most important, according to Google's former senior vice president of operations, Laszlo Bock, is humility.[7] Google has said it tries to weed out arrogant, self-centered people who think they know it all. It strives to hire "learning animals" and let them learn.

Google's culture evidences a belief that the right people will do amazing work if you meet their needs for autonomy and effectiveness by creating an empowering "yes" environment where it's psychologically safe to fail, disagree, tell the truth, ask the tough questions, debate, and take risks. Google employees have an obligation to dissent if they disagree. Keeping quiet is countercultural. Google operates as an idea meritocracy where data, not the HiPPO (highest paid person's opinion), drive decisions. Google believes that employees will find work more meaningful if they have a "voice." Notice how this is a culture designed to provide autonomy, mitigate fear, and promote Psychological Safety.

Google embraces the "messiness" in collaboration. At Google, collaboration is based on three principles: inclusiveness, cooperation, and equality.[8] Every relevant voice is heard and valued. Again, that's autonomy. Google also embraces transparency. Technology and product information are available to everybody. Every employee publishes her or his personal objectives and desired key results so that everyone can understand what's meaningful to the people they work with. Offices are designed to maximize energy and human interaction—to build "relatedness" at work.

To focus managers on helping their direct reports perform and do the "messy" parts well, Google de-emphasizes hierarchy by taking away from managers the authority to hire, fire, rate performance, and determine compensation and promotions. Instead, those responsibilities are in the hands of either peers or independent committees. One key purpose here is to enable Psychological Safety in teams by preventing managers from doling out "work" punishment. It also emphasizes that the manager's role is to serve her or his team and to empower people by helping them achieve their goals. Google wants its managers to be good enablers, not good enforcers. Moreover, Google accepts the fact that innovation requires failure—in fact, it exhorts its people to "fail well" by learning from their failures.[9] The company also takes care in quickly moving people who have worked on failed projects to new good assignments. It believes in organizing around small teams and in giving employees time and choice in their work.

Google, like other hyperlearning organizations, has a strong culture, and it has extensive processes for hiring, running meetings, and innovation. Its hiring, promotion, and compensation processes are designed to mitigate biases, and the hiring process is peer based, with decisions made by committees, not individuals. Google has the most extensive hiring process of any company we have studied. In *Work Rules*, Bock says that Google looks at between one and three million résumés a year and hires only 0.25 percent of the people who apply. It spends lots of money and time finding the right people. Is Google perfect in its hiring? No. But it has an internal research team focused on how to improve hiring and how to help people achieve "competence" and be successful at Google.

A powerful example of that research was published on Google's blog by a company analyst in a 2015 post titled "The Five Keys to a Successful Google Team." Like good researchers, they had a hypothesis. They believed that the right mix of individual traits and skills was the most important aspect for creating a great team. And because they were thinking like scientists, being open-minded and willing to follow the truth wherever it took them, they found that their hypothesis was wrong. Instead, they discovered that how team members interact was much more important. Moreover, the key factor regarding team effectiveness by a material margin was Psychological Safety—whether team members felt safe taking risks and being vulnerable in front of teammates. And it turns out that employees who work on teams that have Psychological Safety are more likely to stay at Google and are more effective and productive. Wow—that's powerful.

Google is very advanced in making its "people function" (human resources) a data-driven science. Its hiring, employee review, and compensation and promotion processes are all data based. Google invests a lot of money in its people function because hiring the right people who have the potential to be high-performing "Googlers" is the most important job a company can do. Google strives to hire people who are dissatisfied with the status quo; have a bias for action; are curious and have the courage to try new things and fail; and embrace Google's duty to dissent yet be a team player. It puts those people in a culture that is egalitarian (except for pay) and that gives people permission to speak freely and to fail. It's a culture that values transparency and openness. It's an idea meritocracy in which data drive decisions and people are given freedom to explore.

Is Google people-centric? We believe so. Does it strive for Psychological Safety and to meet its employees' needs for Self-Determination? We believe it does. Ed visited Google's headquarters a few years ago. Compared with visiting industrial companies or defense contractors or investment banks, it was a completely different experience. Yes, the food and perks were awesome. Yes, the dress code was quite casual. Yes, there were lots of young people. But what was really so different was the energy level, the way in which the work space was designed to promote engaging and collaborating with others, and the very obvious devaluation of hierarchy and elitism of managers. The people he met were refreshingly open and willing to answer any question. There was an intensity that was not motivated by fear. In the halls and break areas, Ed talked to people who were not on his meeting list, and they shared how it felt to work at Google.

### Pixar's Creative Hyperlearning Environment

We first discussed Pixar's cofounder and CEO Ed Catmull in chapter 2 in connection with his NewSmart admonitions that "we are not our ideas" and "our mental models are not reality." Catmull's personal mission in building Pixar was to create an organization that enabled the highest levels of human creativity. To do that, Catmull had to create an environment that inspired and enabled creative types to create and that required a positive emotional environment where it was safe to try, safe to "not cling," and safe to dare to tell captivating stories in innovative new ways.[10]

To be that daring takes courage and trust in your team, your processes, and your training. It also takes feeling that you're in a good place with others who will do you no harm and understand what it's like to do novel things and put yourself out there. It takes an environment of Psychological Safety that promotes candor, permission to speak freely, and permission to make mistakes, and that mitigates the multiple types of fears that we have talked about. What we find so compelling about Catmull's story in *Creativity, Inc.* is that it showed he believes and accepts the reality that the job is never done—that you can't take creativity, candor, and the courage to push one's limits for granted. And you can never completely eradicate fear. He believes that there are unseen and unknown inhibitors that today impede Pixar's creativity and that his job and the job of other leaders and managers is to find those inhibitors and mitigate them.

He doesn't believe that Pixar can maintain its creative excellence if it assumes that it has found the "secret sauce." It has to be vigilant, day in and day out, in warding off complacency, fighting candor slippage, and mitigating fear. There's an intensity at Pixar, according to Catmull, not to lose the rigor of doing the messy parts of creativity—to continually seek out and subject your creative work to review by others in order to improve it. As Catmull explained, at Pixar feedback is additive and provides new information—just like the results of doing an experiment.[11]

Analogizing feedback to the results of scientific experiments is quite helpful. Many times the result of the experiment is different than you expected. It's from these surprises that you modify and improve your hypothesis. Science advances step-by-step through learning from experiments, which is nothing more than constructive feedback. Similarly, when we receive feedback from people we trust who share our mission, it's also additive. When we willingly submit our work to others we trust and ask for their candid feedback, we similarly are open to modifying and improving our ideas. By contrast, if you interpret feedback about your work personally and defensively, you won't be open to learning how to make your work better—you won't be NewSmart, that is, defining yourself by the quality of your thinking, listening, relating, and collaborating. Like Google, Pixar has a people-centric culture that meets its employees' needs for Self-Determination. Its culture focuses on candor, permission to fail, humility, empathy, compassion, and helping people have both a good work life and a healthy personal life. Meaningful work and relationships are the foundation of Pixar's approach. People have autonomy to do their work, "own" their work, and be effective. At Pixar, everyone has a voice.[12] Also like Google, Pixar confronts head-on the need for candor and Psychological Safety and the fact that creative work, just like innovation, happens through an iterative learning process in which one must embrace Humility and not be emotionally defensive.

One of Pixar's feedback processes is the Braintrust, where the senior leaders meet with the creators to analyze their work. This is a candid critique of the work, not the person. What's different from many senior feedback reviews is that the Braintrust has no power or authority. It's advisory. It's up to the creative team to weigh the feedback and to decide what to adopt or reject. Similar to the role of the Google manager, the purpose of Pixar's Braintrust is to identify issues and make suggestions for improvements, for solving problems, and for removing roadblocks.

Through its culture, leadership behaviors, and processes, Pixar strives to maintain the kind of emotionally positive learning environment that provides Psychological Safety and meets Self-Determination needs. Its processes are designed to require collaboration, to have work reviewed by others daily, and to engage in postmortems. Its culture embraces transparency, permission to speak freely regardless of tenure or rank, and permission to fail so long as you learn. Pixar's leaders and managers subject themselves to the same level of reviews and candid feedback as everyone else. Because everyone is held to the same standards and processes, people are more willing to receive feedback with an open mind and to give others such feedback in a way that doesn't attack the other person. Everyone can empathize with others during the review processes because they experience it daily, too. At Pixar, says Catmull, "candor isn't cruel."[13]

Catmull's take on failure is that if you aren't experiencing it, "then you are making a far worse mistake—you are being driven by the desire to avoid it."[14] According to Catmull, the company has a dual approach to failure: acknowledge that it hurt and then acknowledge that failure is a necessary step in reaching excellence—of learning by experimentation. Catmull said that he looks at creative failures as just like learning how to ride a bicycle.[15] By definition, if you're trying to do something innovative or creative, you're trying to do something that is for you a "new thing." So why would you expect to get it right the first time or quickly? Think back to when you learned to ride a bike. Did you just get on a big bicycle and ride it well the first time? We guess that your answer is no. How did you learn? Some of us started with training wheels. Others may have started with a small bicycle—one that was not that tall so the distance to the ground was short. And then you got on and tried. And it probably took some tries before you figured it out.

Pixar has another good lesson for all of us: Conflict and disagreements are good.[16] In fact, to reach the highest levels of thinking we have to have disagreements and we have to resolve disagreements openly and candidly. The messiness of talking out disagreements and being open to subjecting what we believe to critique by others, and being open to understanding what and why other people believe something different than what we believe, is a required process for reaching the best results at Pixar. Note how in this way Pixar provides an environment that enables its people to embrace NewSmart.

Pixar's emphasis on the benefits of disagreements and the necessity of having nonthreatening processes to resolve those differences is directly contrary to the unwritten rules in many organizations: don't disagree with the powerful people; to get along you must go along; and don't rock the boat. Both Pixar's and Google's systems are designed to provide Positivity, Self-Determination, and Psychological Safety, so their people will explore venturing into new areas, asking why, and challenging existing ways. Both cultures are designed to combat our fears of making mistakes, failing, looking stupid, not being liked, and being punished or hurt by others. We believe that they are indicative of what the organization of the future will look like. They are NewSmart organizations.

## The Importance of Processes

The best NewSmart organizations all understand the importance of having and using processes. Pixar's unique feedback, Bridgewater's Radical Transparency, and Intuit's Rapid Experimentation are what enable and promote NewSmart Behaviors and cultivate Positivity, Self-Determination, and Psychological Safety. At a NewSmart organization, processes must be designed to help people behave in ways that result in continuous learning and the highest levels of performing the four SMA Skills. The organization's system must include processes that drive critical thinking, innovative thinking, listening reflectively, mindfulness, collaboration, experimentation, hiring, human development, feedback, rules of engagement, and after-action reviews. Processes are important because they help us overcome our automatic cognitive and emotional proclivities and can help reduce the limiting impacts of ego and fear. Processes help us avoid automatically reverting to our system 1 thinking and listening modes and to our reflexive, emotionally defensive modes. The rigorous daily use of processes was found in every hyperlearning organization we studied.

Learning, innovation, value creation, and excellence all result from behaviors. If you want to change yourself or a team or an organization, we recommend that you focus first on defining the behaviors that you want to change or that you want to emphasize or add. How we think, how we listen, how we connect and relate, how we collaborate, how we manage our thinking, emotions, and behaviors, and how we attend to the world all determine our effectiveness and the effectiveness of our teams and organizations. Behavior is daily; behavior is personal; and behavior has to be measured and owned.

And behaviors start at the top. If the CEO and senior leadership team do not embrace the concepts we've discussed and role-model the desired behaviors, the organization will suboptimize its performance and its ability to stay relevant and competitive in the SMA. In every hyperlearning organization we studied, the senior leadership and CEO role-modeled the desired behaviors. Many times in Ed's executive education and consulting experiences, CEOs have said to him: "I need you to fix my people." Ed's response has always been: "Are you willing to fix yourself, too?"

Herbert A. Simon, one of the founders of Carnegie Mellon's business school and a Nobel Laureate, discussed business management so aptly in his autobiography:

The principles of good management are simple, even trivial. They are not widely practiced for the same reason Christianity is not widely practiced. It is not enough to know what the principles are; you must acquire deeply ingrained habits of carrying them out, in the face of all sorts of strong urges to stray onto more comfortable and pleasant paths.[17]

That is the ultimate challenge for humans in the SMA: to have the self-discipline daily to do the work to excel at the four SMA Skills. Embracing NewSmart and the Humility mindset and practicing the NewSmart Behaviors are a start, but we must also acknowledge and accept that engaging in the type of "messy" human activity necessary to create the highest levels of human thinking, innovating, and creating is not always comfortable or pleasant. Subjecting our thinking to daily critique may not always be comfortable. It won't be comfortable to disagree respectfully with the crowd or higher-ups, own our mistakes, face our fears, or manage our ego. People need help to stay the path. That help can come from the organization's culture, processes, and leadership role modeling, as well as from empathetic teammates who know the difficulty and who know they'll need each other's empathy about the same issues, too.

The journey we see coming for human excellence in the SMA is not efficient, nor does it happen easily or quickly become second nature, because it requires us to go against evolutionary conditioning as well as more recent cultural norms and pressures. Nonetheless, we know it can be done because we have seen it done. We believe that the best-performing organizations in the coming decades will be those that are hyperfocused on developing their people and helping them to achieve human excellence. These organizations will be places where people will have the opportunity to reach their highest potential.

# Your NewSmart Organizational Assessment Tool

Organizations like Google, Pixar, Bridgewater Associates, Starbucks, United Parcel Service, Sysco, W. L. Gore & Associates, IDEO, Southwest Airlines, the US Marine Corps, and the San Antonio Spurs have built systems to drive the desired behaviors to achieve their strategic missions. All are people-centric, high-performance, high-employee-engagement organizations. We believe that people-centricity and high employee engagement are necessary to take an organization to the highest levels of human excellence. That requires Positivity, meeting employees' Self-Determination needs, and Psychological Safety, along with a commitment to continuous iterative learning and human development.

Where do you start? Here's what we recommend:

1. Identify the specific mindsets and behaviors that you want to enable and promote.
2. Design an organizational system that enables and promotes those behaviors. By *system* we mean an organization's structure, culture, human resource policies, leadership behaviors, measurements, rewards, and pro-

cesses. This system must be aligned and seamless to send consistent messages.

3. Note that processes are necessary—they facilitate self-discipline and help mitigate human autopilot tendencies.

Here's a short-version checklist of what we believe are the key NewSmart organizational building blocks. As you read them, we suggest that you grade your organization on each item.

*A = Very Good  B = Good  C = Fair  D = Poor  F = Very Poor*

## Culture

1. Is humanistic and people-centric
2. Enables continuous learning and personal development
3. Provides a team culture, not a "star" culture
4. Devalues elitism and hierarchy—except for compensation
5. Values candor and confronting the brutal facts
6. Serves as an idea meritocracy, with data-driven decision making
7. Provides an emotionally positive work environment
8. Ensures "permission to speak freely"
9. Imposes a duty to constructively debate, challenge the status quo, and dissent
10. Provides Psychological Safety
11. Mitigates ego
12. Mitigates fear (e.g., through postmortems, speaking up, doing learning experiments, and engaging in rigorous thinking processes)
13. Devalues knowing and values "not knowing" and how to learn

14. Favors collaboration over internal competition
15. Has a people-centric leadership model
16. Embraces Humility
17. Provides for mutual accountability

## Behaviors Enabled and Encouraged

1. Humility (quiet egos)
2. Mindfulness
3. Open-mindedness
4. Empathy and compassion
5. Reflective Listening
6. Managing one's thinking
7. Managing one's emotions
8. Emotionally connecting, relating, and engaging with others
9. Embracing change, ambiguity, and new challenges
10. Being truthful and treating others with respect and dignity
11. Seeking feedback and striving daily to improve
12. Self-discipline
13. Mutual accountability
14. Transparent collaboration, not competition

## High Employee Engagement and Development Model

1. Self-Determination needs are met.
2. Every employee has a behavioral-based personal development plan.
3. Leaders and managers are measured and rewarded for developing people.
4. Every employee has a developmental mentor who has no "power" over the employee.

## Processes Used

1. Rigorous hiring for cultural fit
2. Real-time feedback
3. Transparent, fair, and consistently applied reward and promotion policies
4. Measurement of behaviors, not just financial results
5. Measurement of learning—speed and quality
6. Meeting management
7. Critical thinking
8. Creative and innovative thinking
9. Rapid Experimentation
10. Collaboration
11. Reflective Listening
12. After-action reviews
13. PreMortems
14. Mental rehearsal visualization
15. Managing fear
16. 360-degree reviews

# Epilogue

# Our Invitation to You

Our purpose in writing this book is to invite you to consider a new way of thinking and behaving—a new "story"—for the SMA. Our story has two heroes, NewSmart and Humility, and four supporting actors—the NewSmart Behaviors. No matter how you work or where you work, we believe that accepting NewSmart and the Humility mindset and embracing the NewSmart Behaviors will be necessary for you to excel cognitively and emotionally in the SMA and thus increase your chances of being successful in a world transformed by technology.

If you're a manager of a team or leader of an organization, we believe that this book applies to how you lead and engage others in the pursuit of organizational excellence and value creation. The organization of the future is likely to be a NewSmart organization with a humanistic, emotionally positive, collaborative work environment in which individual learning and development drives value creation for multiple stakeholders. Helping people grow and improve personally will be one of your primary responsibilities. It'll be hard to do that for others if you're not also doing it yourself.

Coming technology advances in such areas as smart robots, artificially intelligent smart machines, the Internet of Things, biomedical and genetic engineering, additive manufacturing, nanotechnology, quantum computing, and virtual reality will challenge our humanness, our organizations, and our society. All of us and our children and grandchildren can be served by a new mental model and the behaviors that enable the highest levels of human thinking, learning, emotionally engaging with others, and making meaning together as we all try to navigate a volatile new world that may seem farfetched but is likely to be upon us within the decade.

We invite you to begin implementing your NewSmart Behaviors Personal Improvement Plan so you'll have a better chance of creating meaningful work and meaningful relationships in a world driven by ever-advancing technology. You have the choice to break the chains of automaticity, to quiet your ego, to listen reflectively, to manage your thinking and emotions, and to emotionally connect and relate to others in order to reach your full human potential in the SMA.

Aristotle is reputed to have said it this way: "We are what we repeatedly do. Excellence, then, is not an act, but a habit."

Our warmest regards and best wishes are with you on your journey to human excellence.

—ed and Katherine

# Notes

## Introduction

1  A discussion of historical workplace automation and its impact on the meaning of work and the role of management can be found in Shoshana Zuboff's book *In the Age of the Smart Machine: The Future of Work and Power* (New York: Basic Books, 1988).

2  Erik Brynjolfsson and Andrew McAfee, *The Second Machine Age: Work, Progress, and Prosperity in a Time of Brilliant Technologies* (New York: Norton, 2014), 132.

3  Martin Ford, *Rise of the Robots: Technology and the Threat of a Jobless Future* (New York: Basic, 2015), xi.

4  Ibid.

5  Elaine Pofeldt, "Shocker: Forty Percent of Workers Now Have 'Contingent' Jobs, Says U.S. Government," *Forbes*, May 25, 2015.

6  Carl Benedikt Frey and Michael A. Osborne, "The Future of Employment: How Susceptible Are Jobs to Computerisation?," Oxford Martin School Working Paper, Oxford University, September 17, 2013, http://www.oxfordmartin.ox.ac.uk/downloads/academic/The_Future_of_Employment.pdf; Steve Goldstein, "Eighty Million U.S. Jobs at Risk from Automation, Central Bank Official Says," *Marketwatch*, November 12, 2015, www.marketwatch.com.

7  John A. Bargh and Tanya L. Chartrand, "The Unbearable Automaticity of Being," *American Psychologist* 54, no. 7 (1999): 462–79; Dolly Chugh and Max H. Bazerman, "Bounded Awareness: What You Fail to See Can Hurt You," *Mind & Society* 6, no. 1 (2007): 1–18; Gerald L. Clore and Janet Palmer, "Affective Guidance of Intelligent Agents: How Emotion Controls Cognition," *Cognitive Systems Research* 10, no. 1 (2009): 21–30; Antonio Damasio, *Descartes' Error: Emotion, Reason, and the Human Brain* (New York: Penguin, 1994); Daniel Kahneman, "Bias, Blindness, and How We Truly Think (Part 1)," Bloomberg.com, October 24, 2011; Kahneman, "A Short

Course in Thinking about Thinking," Edge Master Class, Edge.org, Rutherford, CA, July 20–22, 2007, www.edge.org/; Daniel Kahneman and Gary Klein, "Conditions for Intuitive Expertise: A Failure to Disagree," *American Psychologist* 64, no. 6 (2009): 515–26; Elizabeth A. Phelps, "Emotion and Cognition: Insights from Studies of the Human Amygdala," *Annual Review of Psychology* 57 (2006): 27–53; Ron Ritchhart and David N. Perkins, "Learning to Think: The Challenges of Teaching Thinking," in *The Cambridge Handbook of Thinking and Reasoning*, ed. Keith J. Holyoak and Robert G. Morrison (Cambridge: Cambridge University Press, 2005); Justin Storbeck and Gerald L. Clore, "On the Interdependence of Cognition and Emotion," *Cognition and Emotion* 21, no. 6 (2007): 1212–37; Amos Tversky and Daniel Kahneman, "Judgment under Uncertainty: Heuristics and Biases," *Science* 185 (1974): 1124–31.

8  Chris Argyris, "Teaching Smart People How to Learn," *Harvard Business Review* 69, no. 3 (1991): 99–109; Jack Mezirow, "Transformative Learning: Theory to Practice," *New Directions for Adult and Continuing Education* 74 (1997): 5–12; Abraham H. Maslow, *Toward a Psychology of Being* (Princeton, NJ: D. Van Nostrand, 1962); Richard J. Davidson and Sharon Begley, *The Emotional Life of Your Brain: How Its Unique Patterns Affect the Way You Think, Feel, and Live—and How You Can Change Them* (New York: Plume, 2013).

9  Barbara Fredrickson, *Love 2.0: How Our Supreme Emotion Affects Everything We Feel, Think, Do, and Become* (New York: Penguin, 2013), 10.

10  Jerry Kaplan, *Humans Need Not Apply: A Guide to Wealth and Work in the Age of Artificial Intelligence* (New Haven, CT: Yale University Press, 2015).

## Chapter I The Smart Machine Age: A New Game Requires New Rules

1  Richard Feloni, "Billionaire Hedge Fund Manager Ray Dalio—Who Encourages Employees to See Their Team as a 'Machine'—Is Building an Artificial Intelligence Unit," *Business Insider,* February 27, 2015; Jonathan Cohn, "The Robot Will See You Now," *Atlantic,* February 20, 2013.

2  Peter Diamandis, "Disrupting Today's Healthcare System," *Huffington Post,* November 9, 2015.

3  Barb Darrow, "Computers Can't Read Your Mind Yet, but They're Getting Closer," *Fortune,* September 11, 2015.

4  Frank MacCrory, George Westerman, Yousef Alhammadi, and Erik Brynjolfsson, "Racing with and against the Machine: Changes in Occupational Skill Composition in an Era of Rapid Technological Advance," Thirty-Fifth International Conference on Information Systems, Auckland, December 14–17, 2014, 14.

5  Choe Sang-Hun, "Google's Computer Program Beats Lee Se-dol in Go Tournament," *New York Times,* March 15, 2016.

6  See, for example, Ford, *Rise of the Robots*; Carl Benedikt Frey and Michael Osburn, "Technology at Work: The Future of Innovation and Employment," Citi GPS:

Global Perspectives & Solutions, February 2015, www.oxfordmartin.ox.ac.uk; Brynjolfsson and McAfee, *Second Machine Age: Work*; David Hémous and Morten Olsen, "The Rise of the Machines: Automation, Horizontal Innovation, and Income Inequality," IESE Business School Working Paper No. WP1110-E, December 8, 2014, http://papers.ssrn.com/sol3/papers.cfm?abstract_id=2328774; J. D. Heyes, "Robots to Take Over Jobs in Human Service Industry, Increasing the Percentage of Unemployed Americans," *Natural News*, April 3, 2013, www.naturalnews.com; "Immigrants from the Future," *Economist*, March 29, 2014; "Rise of the Robots," *Economist*, March 29, 2014; Cohn, "The Robot Will See You Now"; "The Disruptive Era of Smart Machines Is upon Us," Gartner report, September 30, 2013; Adam Clark Estes, "Meet Google's Robot Army. It's Growing," *Gizmodo*, January 27, 2014, gizmodo.com; Seth G. Benzell, Laurence J. Kotlikoff, Guillermo LaGarda, and Jeffrey D. Sachs, "Robots Are Us: Some Economics of Human Replacement," NBER Working Paper No. 20941, National Bureau of Economic Research, Cambridge, MA, February 2015.

7   "Amazon's Bezos: It's Hard to Overstate Impact of AI," May 31, 2016, www.msn.com/en-us/video/tunedin/amazons-bezos-hard-to-overstate-impact-of-ai/vp-BBtJTKz.

8   "What's Next for Artificial Intelligence: The Best Minds in the Business … on What Life Will Look Like in the Age of the Machines," *Wall Street Journal*, June 14, 2016.

9   Kevin Kelly, *The Inevitable: Understanding the 12 Technological Forces That Will Shape Our Future* (New York: Viking, 2016), 21.

10   Goldstein, "Eighty Million U.S. Jobs at Risk from Automation."

11   Frey and Osborne, "Future of Employment."

12   Pofeldt, "Shocker: Forty Percent of Workers Now Have 'Contingent' Jobs."

13   Ryan Kim, "By 2020, Independent Workers Will Be the Majority," Gigaom, December 8, 2011, gigaom.com/2011/12/08/mbo-partners-network-2011/.

14   Ford, *Rise of the Robots*, 176

15   Tony Wagner, *Most Likely to Succeed: Preparing Our Kids for the Innovation Era* (New York: Scribner, 2015), 63.

16   Howard Gardner, *Five Minds for the Future* (Boston: Harvard Business Press, 2006).

17   See, e.g., "New Vision for Education: Unlocking the Potential of Technology," World Economic Forum and Boston Consulting Group, Geneva, Switzerland (2015); MacCrory, Westerman, Alhammadi, and Brynjolfsson, "Racing with and against the Machine."

18   Daniel T. Willingham, "Critical Thinking: Why Is It So Hard to Teach?" *Arts Education Policy Review* 109, no. 4 (2008): 21–32.

19   Daniel Kahneman, *Thinking, Fast and Slow* (New York: Farrar, Straus and Giroux, 2011), 14.

20   Ibid., 24.

21   Ibid.

22  Ibid., 3.

23  Herbert Simon, *Models of My Life* (Cambridge: MIT Press, 1996), 144.

24  Gerald L. Clore and Jeffrey R. Huntsinger, "How Emotions Inform Judgment and Regulate Thought," *Trends in Cognitive Science* 11, no. 9 (2007): 393–99; Gerald L. Clore and Janet Palmer, "Affective Guidance of Intelligent Agents: How Emotion Controls Cognition," *Cognitive Systems Research* 10, no. 1 (2009): 21–30; Antonio R. Damasio, "Descartes' Error and the Future of Human Life," *Scientific American* 271, no. 4 (1994): 144; Jan De Houwer and Dirk Hermans, eds., *Cognition and Emotion: Reviews of Current Research and Theories* (Hove, UK: Psychology Press, 2010); Mary Helen Immordino-Yang, "The Smoke around Mirror Neurons: Goals as Sociocultural and Emotional Organizers of Perception and Action in Learning," *Mind, Brain, and Education* 2, no. 2 (2008): 67–73; Mary Helen Immordino-Yang, Joanna A. Christodoulou, and Vanessa Singh, "Rest Is Not Idleness: Implications of the Brain's Default Mode for Human Development and Education," *Perspectives on Psychological Science* 7, no. 4 (2012): 352–64; Mary Helen Immordino-Yang and Antonio Damasio, "We Feel, Therefore We Learn: The Relevance of Affective and Social Neuroscience to Education," *Mind, Brain, and Education* 1, no. 1 (2007): 3–10; Mary Helen Immordino-Yang and Kurt W. Fischer, "Neuroscience Bases of Learning," in *International Encyclopedia of Education,* 3rd ed., ed. V. G. Aukrust (Oxford: Elsevier, 2009); Nasir Naqvi, Baba Shiv, and Antoine Bechara, "The Role of Emotion in Decision Making: A Cognitive Neuroscience Perspective," *Current Directions in Psychological Science* 15, no. 5 (2006): 260–64; Mike Oaksford, Frances Morris, Becki Grainger, and J. Mark G. Williams, "Mood, Reasoning, and Central Executive Processes," *Journal of Experimental Psychology: Learning, Memory, and Cognition* 22, no. 2 (1996): 476–92; Luiz Pessoa, "Emergent Processes in Cognitive-Emotional Interactions," *Dialogues in Clinical Neuroscience* 12, no. 4 (2010): 433–48; Pessoa, "How Do Emotion and Motivation Direct Executive Control?" *Trends in Cognitive Sciences* 13, no. 4 (2009): 160–66; Pessoa, "On the Relationship between Emotion and Cognition," *Nature Reviews/Neuroscience* 9 (2008): 148–58; Justin Storbeck and Gerald L. Clore, "On the Interdependence of Cognition and Emotion," *Cognition and Emotion* 21, no. 6 (2007): 1212–37.

25  Karen Gasper, "Do You See What I See? Affect and Visual Information Processing," *Cognition and Emotion* 18, no. 3 (2004): 405–21; Gasper, "Permission to Seek Freely? The Effect of Happy and Sad Moods on Generating Old and New Ideas," *Creativity Research Journal* 16, nos. 2–3 (2004): 215–29; Gasper, "When Necessity Is the Mother of Invention: Mood and Problem Solving," *Journal of Experimental Social Psychology* 39, no. 3 (2003): 248–62; Karen Gasper and Gerald L. Clore, "Attending to the Big Picture: Mood and Global versus Local Processing of Visual Information," *Psychological Science* 13, no. 1 (2002): 34–40; Barbara L. Fredrickson, "Updated Thinking on Positivity Ratios," *American Psychologist* 68, no. 9 (2013): 814–22; Barbara L. Fredrickson, *Positivity: Groundbreaking Research Reveals How to Embrace*

*the Hidden Strength of Positive Emotions, Overcome Negativity, and Thrive* (New York: Crown, 2009); Fredrickson, "The Role of Positive Emotions in Positive Psychology: The Broaden-and-Build Theory of Positive Emotions," *American Psychologist* 56, no. 3 (2001): 218–26; Barbara L. Fredrickson and Christine Branigan, "Positive Emotions Broaden the Scope of Attention and Thought-Action Repertoires," *Cognition and Emotion* 19, no. 3 (2005): 313–32.

26 Daniel Dennett, *Intuition Pumps and Other Tools for Thinking* (New York: Norton, 2013), 21.

27 Pietro Badia, Bonnie McBane, and Steve Suter, "Preference Behavior in an Immediate versus Variably Delayed Shock Situation with and without a Warning Signal," *Journal of Experimental Psychology* 72, no. 6 (1966): 847–52.

28 Roy Baumeister and Mark Leary, "The Need to Belong: Desire for Interpersonal Attachments as a Fundamental Human Motivation," *Psychological Bulletin* 117, no. 3 (1995): 497–529.

29 Geoff Colvin, *Humans Are Underrated: What High Achievers Know That Brilliant Machines Never Will* (New York: Portfolio, 2015).

## Chapter 2 NewSmart: A New Definition of "Smart"

1 Jack Mezirow, "Transformative Learning: Theory to Practice," *New Directions for Adult and Continuing Education* 74 (Summer 1997): 5.

2 Ibid., 7.

3 Ed Catmull and Amy Wallace, *Creativity, Inc.: Overcoming the Unseen Forces That Stand in the Way of True Inspiration* (New York: Random House, 2014), 94.

4 Ibid., 182.

5 Ray Dalio, Principles, Bridgewater Associates, www.bwater.com/Uploads/File-Manager/Principles/Bridgewater-Associates-Ray-Dalio-Principles.pdf.

6 Edward D. Hess, *Learn or Die: Using Science to Build a Leading-Edge Learning Organization* (New York: Columbia University Press, 2014).

7 Ray Dalio, "How to Get a Job ... at Bridgewater," Bloomberg.com, April 12, 2012.

8 Hess, *Learn or Die*, 122–26.

9 Stuart Firestein, *Ignorance: How It Drives Science* (Oxford: Oxford University Press, 2012), 15.

10 Kahneman, *Thinking, Fast and Slow*, 14.

11 Christopher Peterson and Martin E.P. Seligman, *Character Strengths and Virtues: A Handbook and Classification* (Oxford: Oxford University Press, 2004), 144.

12 Mark Pagel, "Knowledge as Hypothesis," in *This Will Make You Smarter: New Scientific Concepts to Improve Your Thinking*, ed. John Brockman (New York: Harper Perennial, 2012), 341.

13 Max Tegmark, "Promoting a Scientific Lifestyle," in Brockman, *This Will Make You Smarter*, 20.

14 Carlo Rovelli, " The Uselessness of Certainty," in Brockman, *This Will Make You*

*Smarter*, 51.

15  Paul and Elder, *Critical Thinking*, 33.

16  Steven Johnson, *Where Good Ideas Come From: The Natural History of Innovation* (New York: Riverhead, 2010), 134.

17  Mihaly Csikszentmihalyi, *Creativity: Flow and the Psychology of Discovery and Invention* (New York: Harper Perennial, 1997), 11.

18  Brené Brown, *Daring Greatly: How the Courage to Be Vulnerable Transforms the Way We Live, Love, Parent, and Lead* (New York: Avery, 2012), 130.

19  Ibid.

20  Carol S. Dweck, *Mindset: The New Psychology of Success* (New York: Ballantine, 2006), 175.

21  Tom Kelley and David Kelley, *Creative Confidence: Unleashing the Creative Potential within Us All* (New York: Crown Business, 2013), 51.

## Chapter 3  Humility: The Gateway to Human Excellence in the SMA

1  "Valuable Intellectual Traits," CriticalThinking.org, www.criticalthinking.org/pages/valuable-intellectual-traits/528.

2  Jean M. Twenge and W. Keith Campbell, *The Narcissism Epidemic: Living in the Age of Entitlement* (New York: Atria, 2009).

3  W. Keith Campbell and Constantine Sedikides, "Self-Threat Magnifies the Self-Serving Bias: A Meta-Analytic Integration," *Review of General Psychology* 3, no. 1 (1999): 23; Miron Zuckerman, "Attribution of Success and Failure Revisited, or: The Motivational Bias Is Alive and Well in Attribution Theory," *Journal of Personality* 47, no. 2 (1979): 245–87.

4  Roger G. Tweed and Darrin R. Lehman,"Learning Considered Within a Cultural Context: Confucian and Socratic Approaches," *American Psychologist* 57, no. 2 (2002): 95.

5  For an overview of recent research, see Joseph Chancellor and Sonja Lyubomirsky, "Humble Beginnings: Current Trends, State Perspective, and Hallmarks of Humility," *Social and Personality Psychology Compass* 7, no. 11 (2013): 819–33.

6  P. Z. Myers, "The Mediocrity Principle," in Brockman, *This Will Make You Smarter*, 6.

7  Frans de Waal, "What I Learned from Tickling Apes," *New York Times*, April 8, 2016, .

8  Adam Grant, *Give and Take: Why Helping Others Drives Our Success* (New York: Penguin, 2014).

9  Jim Collins, *Good to Great: Why Some Companies Make the Leap ... and Others Don't* (New York: HarperBusiness, 2001), 22.

10  Douglas LaBier, "Why Humble, Empathic Business Leaders Are More Successful," *Huffington Post*, December 24, 2014; Karoline Hofslett Kopperud, "Engaging Leaders in the Eyes of the Beholder on the Relationship between Transformational

Leadership, Work Engagement, Service Climate, and Self–Other Agreement," *Journal of Leadership & Organizational Studies* 21, no. 1 (2014): 29–42; Bradley P. Owens, "Expressed Humility in Organizations: Implications for Performance, Teams, and Leadership," *Organization Science* 24, no. 5 (2013): 1517–38.

11 See, for example, Adam Bryant, *Quick and Nimble: Lessons from Leading CEOs on How to Create a Culture of Innovation* (New York: Times Books, 2014); Hess, *Learn or Die*.

12 Edward D. Hess, *The Road to Organic Growth: How Great Companies Consistently Grow Marketshare from Within* (New York: McGraw-Hill, 2007), 147.

13 Hess, *Learn or Die*, 18.

14 Ibid.

15 Ibid.

16 Ibid.

17 Laszlo Bock, *Work Rules! Insights from Inside Google That Will Transform How You Live and Lead* (New York: Twelve, 2015).

18 Quoted in Thomas L. Friedman, "How to Get a Job at Google," *New York Times*, February 22, 2014.

19 Ibid.

20 Laszlo Bock, *Work Rules! Insights from Inside Google That Will Transform How You Live and Lead* (New York: Twelve, 2015), 67.

21 Catmull and Wallace, *Creativity, Inc.*, xvi.

22 Jocko Willink and Leif Babin, *Extreme Ownership: How U.S. Navy SEALs Lead and Win* (New York: St. Martin's, 2015), 100.

## Chapter 4  Quieting Ego

1 Walter Mischel, *The Marshmallow Test: Mastering Self-Control* (New York: Little, Brown, 2014), 260.

2 Barbara Fredrickson, *Positivity: Groundbreaking Research Reveals How to Embrace the Hidden Strength of Positive Emotions, Overcome Negativity, and Thrive* (New York: Crown, 2009), 179.

3 Jon Kabat-Zinn, *Wherever You Go, There You Are: Mindfulness Meditation in Everyday Life* (New York: Hyperion, 1994), 4.

4 Matthew A. Killingsworth and Daniel T. Gilbert, "A Wandering Mind Is an Unhappy Mind," *Science* 330, no. 6006 (2010): 932.

5 William James, *The Principles of Psychology*, vol. 1 (New York: Cosimo Classics, 2013), 424.

6 Richard J. Davidson et al., "Alterations in Brain and Immune Function Produced by Mindfulness Meditation," *Psychosomatic Medicine* 65, no. 4 (2003): 564–70; Gaelle Desbordes et al., "Effects of Mindful-Attention and Compassion Meditation Training on Amygdala Response to Emotional Stimuli in an Ordinary, Non-Meditative State," *Frontiers in Human Neuroscience* 6 (2012); Britta K. Hölzel et al., "How Does Mindfulness Meditation Work? Proposing Mechanisms of Action from a Conceptu-

al and Neural Perspective," *Perspectives on Psychological Science* 6, no. 6 (2011): 537–59; Britta K. Hölzel et al., "Mindfulness Practice Leads to Increases in Regional Brain Gray Matter Density," *Psychiatry Research* 191, no. 1 (2011): 36–43; Jon Kabat-Zinn, "Mindfulness-Based Interventions in Context: Past, Present, and Future," *Clinical Psychology: Science and Practice* 10, no. 2 (2003): 144–56; Olga M. Klimecki, Susanne Leiberg, Claus Lamm, and Tania Singer, "Functional Neural Plasticity and Associated Changes in Positive Affect after Compassion Training," *Cerebral Cortex* 23, no. 7 (2013): 1552–61; Amishi P. Jha, Jason Krompinger, and Michael J. Baime, "Mindfulness Training Modifies Subsystems of Attention," *Cognitive, Affective, & Behavioral Neuroscience* 7, no. 2 (2007): 109–19; Amishi P. Jha et al., "Examining the Protective Effects of Mindfulness Training on Working Memory Capacity and Affective Experience," *Emotion* 10, no. 1 (2010): 54–64; Antoine Lutz, Julie Brefczynski-Lewis, Tom Johnstone, and Richard J. Davidson, "Regulation of the Neural Circuitry of Emotion by Compassion Meditation: Effects of Meditative Expertise," *PLOS ONE* 3, no. 3 (2008): e1897; Antoine Lutz, Heleen A. Slagter, John D. Dunne, and Richard J. Davidson, "Attention Regulation and Monitoring in Meditation," *Trends in Cognitive Sciences* 12, no. 4 (2008): 163–69.

7 Badri Bajaj and Neerja Pande, "Mediating Role of Resilience in the Impact of Mindfulness on Life Satisfaction and Affect as Indices of Subjective Well-Being," *Personality and Individual Differences* 93 (2016): 63–67.

8 Mark Williams and Danny Penman, *Mindfulness: An Eight-Week Plan for Finding Peace in a Frantic World* (New York: Rodale, 2011), 5.

9 Ibid., 6; Hölzel et al., "How Does Mindfulness Meditation Work?"; Hölzel et al., "Mindfulness Practice Leads to Increases in Regional Brain Gray Matter Density."

10 Elliott Kruse, Joseph Chancellor, Peter M. Ruberton, and Sonja Lyubomirsky, "An Upward Spiral between Gratitude and Humility," *Social Psychological and Personality Science* 5, no. 7 (2014): 805–14.

11 Barbara Ehrenreich, "The Selfish Side of Gratitude," *New York Times*, December 31, 2015.

## Chapter 5 Managing Self: Thinking and Emotions

1 Hess, *Learn or Die*.

2 Ibid., 81–86.

3 Ibid., 75–78.

4 Gary Klein, *Seeing What Others Don't: The Remarkable Ways We Gain Insights* (New York: PublicAffairs, 2013).

5 Ibid., 86–87.

6 Ibid., 245; Jeanne Liedtka and Tim Ogilvie, *Designing for Growth: A Design Thinking Tool Kit for Managers* (New York: Columbia University Press, 2011).

7 Intuit Labs, "NEXT Tool: Rapid Experiments with Customers," www.intuitlabs. com/portfolio/next-tool/, accessed August 1, 2016.

8 Twyla Tharp, *The Creative Habit: Learn It and Use It for Life* (New York: Simon and Schuster, 2003).

9 R. Keith Sawyer, *Explaining Creativity: The Science of Human Innovation* (New York: Oxford University Press, 2012).

10 Gary Klein, "Performing a Project PreMortem," *Harvard Business Review* 85, no. 9 (2007): 18–19.

11 Ibid.

12 Richard J. Davidson, *The Emotional Life of Your Brain: How Its Unique Patterns Affect the Way You Think, Feel, and Live—and How You Can Change Them* (New York: Plume, 2012), 90.

13 Walter Mischel, *The Marshmallow Test: Mastering Self-Control* (New York: Little, Brown, 2014), 150.

14 Hess, *Learn or Die*, 156.

15 Tharp, *Creative Habit*, 31.

16 Ibid., 21.

17 Kelley and Kelley, *Creative Confidence*, 183.

18 Gregory Berns, *Iconoclast: A Neuroscientist Reveals How to Think Differently* (Boston: Harvard Business Press, 2008), 76–81.

19 Pamela Weintraub, "The Voice of Reason," *Psychology Today*, June 2014, 58.

20 Mischel, *Marshmallow Test*, 260.

21 Peter Salovey and J. D. Mayer, "Emotional Intelligence," *Imagination, Cognition, and Personality* 9 (1990): 189.

22 John D. Mayer and Peter Salovey, "What Is Emotional Intelligence?," in *Emotional Development and Emotional Intelligence: Educational Implications*, ed. Peter Salovey and David J. Sluyter (New York: Basic Books, 1997).

23 Anita Williams Woolley et al., "Evidence for a Collective Intelligence Factor in the Performance of Human Groups," *Science* 330.6004 (2010): 686–88.

24 David Engel et al., "Reading the Mind in the Eyes or Reading between the Lines? Theory of Mind Predicts Collective Intelligence Equally Well Online and Face-to-Face," *PLOS ONE* 9.12 (2014): e115212.

25 Lisa Feldman Barrett, "What Emotions Are and Aren't," *New York Times*, July 31, 2015.

## Chapter 6 Reflective Listening

1 William Isaacs, *Dialogue: The Art of Thinking Together* (New York: Crown Business, 1999), 84.

2 Jane E. Dutton, *Energize Your Workplace: How to Create and Sustain High-Quality Connections at Work* (San Francisco: Jossey-Bass, 2003), 37.

3 Isaacs, *Dialogue*, 101.

4 Ibid., 149.

## Chapter 7  Otherness: Emotionally Connecting and Relating to Others

1 Barbara Fredrickson, *Positivity: Top-notch Research Reveals the 3:1 Ratio That Will Change Your Life* (New York: Three Rivers, 2009), 191.
2 Jane E. Dutton, *Energize Your Workplace: How to Create and Sustain High-Quality Connections at Work* (San Francisco: Jossey-Bass, 2003), 16–17.
3 Sidney M. Jourard, *The Transparent Self* (New York: Van Nostrand Reinhold, 1971), 6.
4 Barbara Fredrickson, *Love 2.0: How Our Supreme Emotion Affects Everything We Feel, Think, Do, and Become* (New York: Penguin, 2013), 10.
5 Edgar H. Schein, *Humble Consulting: How to Provide Real Help Faster* (Oakland, CA: Berrett-Koehler, 2016), 15.
6 Ibid., 23.

## Chapter 8  Your NewSmart Behaviors Assessment Tool

1 Robert Kegan and Lisa Laskow Lahey, *Immunity to Change: How to Overcome It and Unlock the Potential in Yourself and Your Organization* (Boston: Harvard Business Press, 2009).

## Chapter 9: Leading a NewSmart Organization

1 Abraham H. Maslow, *Toward a Psychology of Being*, 3rd ed. (New York: Wiley, 1998), 65.
2 Hess, *Learn or Die.*
3 Paul P. Baard, Edward L. Deci, and Richard M. Ryan, "Intrinsic Need Satisfaction: A Motivational Basis of Performance and Well-Being in Two Work Settings," *Journal of Applied Social Psychology* 34 (2004): 2046; Edward L. Deci and Richard M. Ryan, "The 'What' and 'Why' of Goal Pursuits: Human Needs and the Self-Determination of Behavior," *Psychological Inquiry* 11, no. 4 (2000): 227–68.
4 Richard Feloni, "Facebook's HR Chief Conducted a Company-Wide Study to Find Its Best Managers and Seven Behaviors Stood Out," *Business Insider*, January 27, 2016, www.businessinsider.com/.
5 Adam Grant, *Originals: How Non-Conformists Move the World* (New York: Viking, 2016), 13.
6 Julia B. Bear and Anita Williams Woolley, "The Role of Gender in Team Collaboration and Performance," *Interdisciplinary Science Review* 36, no. 2 (2011): 146–53; Marc A. Brackett, John D. Mayer, and Rebecca M. Warner, "Emotional Intelligence and Its Relation to Everyday Behavior," *Personality and Individual Differences* 36 (2004): 1387–1402; Larry Cahill, "His Brain, Her Brain," *Scientific American Mind*, special collectors' edition 21, no. 2 (2010): 4–11; Cahill, "Why Sex Matters for Neuroscience," *Nature Reviews Neuroscience* 7, no. 6 (2006): 477–84; Emily Grijalva et al., "Gender Differences in Narcissism: A Meta-Analytic Review," *Psychological Bulletin*

141, no. 2 (2015): 261; William Ickes, Paul R. Gesn, and Tiffany Graham, "Gender Differences in Empathic Accuracy: Differential Ability or Differential Motivation?" *Personal Relationships* 7 (2000): 95–109.

7 Bock, *Work Rules!*, 67.
8 Eric Schmidt and Jonathan Rosenberg, *How Google Works* (New York: Grand Central, 2014), 155.
9 Ibid., 237.
10 Catmull and Wallace, *Creativity, Inc.*, 185.
11 Ibid., 101.
12 Ibid., 61.
13 Ibid., 104.
14 Ibid., 109.
15 Ibid.
16 Ibid., 139.
17 Herbert A. Simon, *Models of My Life* (Cambridge, MA: MIT Press, 1996), 150.

# Recommended Reading

Laszlo Bock, *Work Rules! Insights from Inside Google That Will Transform How You Live and Lead* (New York: Twelve, 2015).

Lyle E. Bourne Jr. and Alice F. Healy, *Train Your Mind for Peak Performance: A Science-Based Approach for Achieving Your Goals* (Washington, DC: American Psychological Association, 2013).

David Brooks, *The Road to Character* (New York: Random House, 2015).

Brené Brown, *Daring Greatly: How the Courage to Be Vulnerable Transforms the Way We Live, Love, Parent, and Lead* (New York: Avery, 2012).

Peter C. Brown, Henry L. Roediger III, and Mark McDaniel, *Make It Stick: The Science of Successful Learning* (Cambridge, MA: Belknap Press of Harvard University Press, 2014).

Erik Brynjolfsson and Andrew McAfee, *The Second Machine Age: Work, Progress, and Prosperity in a Time of Brilliant Technologies* (New York: Norton, 2014).

Susan Cain, *The Power of Introverts in a World That Can't Stop Talking* (New York: Crown, 2012).

Ed Catmull and Amy Wallace, *Creativity, Inc.: Overcoming the Unseen Forces That Stand in the Way of True Inspiration* (New York: Random House, 2014).

Jim Collins and Jerry I. Porras, *Successful Habits of Visionary Companies*, 10th rev. ed. (New York: HarperBusiness, 2004).

Richard J. Davidson and Sharon Begley, *The Emotional Life of Your Brain: How Its Unique Patterns Affect the Way You Think, Feel, and Live—and How You Can Change Them* (New York: Hudson Street, 2012).

Jane E. Dutton, *Energize Your Workplace: How to Create and Sustain High-Quality Connections at Work* (San Francisco: Jossey-Bass, 2003).

Carol S. Dweck, *Mindset: The New Psychology of Success* (New York: Ballantine, 2006).

Amy C. Edmondson, *Teaming: How Organizations Learn, Innovate, and Compete in the Knowledge Economy* (San Francisco: Jossey-Bass, 2014).

Anders Ericsson and Robert Pool, *Peak: Secrets from the New Science of Expertise* (New York: Houghton Mifflin Harcourt, 2016).

Martin Ford, *Rise of the Robots: Technology and the Threat of a Jobless Future* (New York: Basic, 2015).

Barbara L. Fredrickson, *Positivity: Groundbreaking Research Reveals How to Embrace the Hidden Strength of Positive Emotions, Overcome Negativity, and Thrive* (New York: Crown, 2009).

Marshall Goldsmith, *What Got You Here Won't Get You There: How Successful People Become Even More Successful* (New York: Hyperion, 2007).

Adam Grant, *Originals: How Non-Conformists Move the World* (New York: Viking, 2016).

Chip Heath and Dan Heath, *Decisive: How to Make Better Choices in Life and Work* (New York: Crown Business, 2013).

Edward D. Hess, *Learn or Die: Using Science to Build a Leading-Edge Learning Organization* (New York: Columbia University Press, 2014).

William Isaacs, *Dialogue: The Art of Thinking Together* (New York: Crown Business, 1999).

Jon Kabat-Zinn, *Mindfulness for Beginners: Reclaiming the Present Moment and Your Life* (Boulder, CO: Sounds True, 2012).

Daniel Kahneman, *Thinking, Fast and Slow* (New York: Farrar, Straus and Giroux, 2011).

David Kelley and Tom Kelley, *Creative Confidence: Unleashing the Creative Potential within Us All* (London: William Collins, 2015).

Gary Klein, *Seeing What Others Don't: The Remarkable Ways We Gain Insights* (New York: PublicAffairs, 2013).

Jeanne Liedtka and Tim Ogilvie, *Designing for Growth: A Design Thinking Tool Kit for Managers* (New York: Columbia University Press, 2011).

Walter Mischel, *The Marshmallow Test: Mastering Self-Control* (New York: Little, Brown, 2014).

Richard Paul and Linda Elder, *Critical Thinking: Tools for Taking Charge of Your Professional and Personal Life* (Upper Saddle River, NJ: Pearson Education, 2014).

Bernard Roth, *The Achievement Habit: Stop Wishing, Start Doing, and Take Command of Your Life* (New York: HarperCollins, 2015).

R. Keith Sawyer, *Explaining Creativity: The Science of Human Innovation* (Oxford: Oxford University Press, 2012).

Edgar H. Schein, *Humble Consulting: How to Provide Real Help Faster* (Oakland, CA: Berrett-Koehler, 2016).

———, *Humble Inquiry: The Gentle Art of Asking Instead of Telling* (San Francisco: Berrett-Koehler, 2013).

Eric Schmidt and Jonathan Rosenthal, *How Google Works* (New York: Grand Central, 2014).

Philip E. Tetlock and Dan Gardner, *Superforecasting: The Art and Science of Prediction* (New York: Crown, 2015).

Twyla Tharp, *The Creative Habit: Learn It and Use It for Life* (New York: Simon and Schuster, 2003).

Tony Wagner, *Most Likely to Succeed: Preparing Our Kids for the Innovation Era* (New York: Scribner, 2015).

Mark Williams and Danny Penman, *Mindfulness: An Eight-Week Plan for Finding Peace in a Frantic World* (New York: Rodale, 2011).

# Acknowledgments

This book's focus on human excellence builds on eight of Ed's other books, and we acknowledge with deep gratitude the help of thousands of leaders and managers of organizations who contributed to that evolutionary history, including Best Buy, Bridgewater Associates, Harris Corporation, Intuit, Levy Restaurants, Investure LLC, Pitney Bowes, Room & Board, Stryker Corporation, Synovous Financial Corp., Sysco Corporation, Tiffany & Co., United Parcel Services, and W. L. Gore & Associates.

We also thank these scholars and researchers who have played key roles in Ed's work: Lyle Bourne Jr., Kim Cameron, Richard D'Aveni, Robert Drazin, Robert Kazanjian, Gary Klein, and Jeanne Liedtka.

Special thanks to Tommy Battle, Bill Berkley, Rob Berkley, Chris Mattis, Fernando Merce, Dr. Pamela Moran, Marvin Riley, Sean Ryan, and Isaac Vanderburg for sharing some of the content of this book with their teams and providing us with the opportunity to iteratively learn and improve our work.

To Jeanne Liedtka, Randy Salzman, our publisher's four reviewers, and Dr. Lyle Bourne Jr.: we thank you for your reviews and constructive feedback, which made this a better book.

To Berrett-Koehler Publishers, Managing Director Jeevan Sivasubramaniam, Editorial Director Neal Maillet, and the entire purpose-driven team at BK: we thank you for your partnership.

Likewise, we are honored and thankful for all the support given to this work by our book publicist Barbara Monteiro and by the excellent Communications and Marketing Team at the Darden Business School, led by Julie Daum.

To Darden Business School and Batten Institute leaders, including Dean Emeritus Bob Bruner, Sean Carr, Jim Freeland, Michael Lenox, Jeanne Liedtka, and Sankaran Venkataraman: we thank you for all your research support and encouragement over the years.

# Index

## A

*Achievement Habit, The* (Roth), 108, 131
Amazon, 18, 97
*Are We Smart Enough to Know How Smart Animals Are?* (De Waal), 66
artificial intelligence (AI), 15, 17, 18–20, 21, 31, 171
automation, 2–4, 15–20, 31, 153–54

## B

Berns, Gregory, 108
Bezos, Jeff, 18, 97–98
Bock, Laszlo, 71, 171, 173
Bourne, Lyle, Jr., 116–17, 143
breathing, 82, 86–87, 106, 145
Bridgewater Associates: critical thinking tools at, 104; Humility as mindset at, 8, 70; ignorance embraced at, 46–47, 51; and mindfulness practice, 85–86; and NewSmart's genesis, 7, 39; organizational system of, as NewSmart, 158, 183; and psychological distancing, 107; Radical Transparency policy, 70, 179
Brown, Brené, 53–54

## C

Catmull, Ed, 7, 44–45, 71–72, 175–78
choice, power of: in behavior, 77, 105; and mindfulness practice, 82, 83, 88–89; and Reflective Listening, 119–20
collaboration: and emotional intelligence, 110, 111–12, 114; at Google, 172; and Humility, 66, 68, 72; and identifying with one's beliefs, 41–42, 43; as "making meaning together," 28, 157; and Reflective Listening, 115; and SMA Skills, 3, 4, 23, 28, 31, 114

Collins, Jim, 69
Colvin, Geoff, 31
Confucious, 48, 63
Cook, Scott, 70
Connor-Davidson Resiliance Scale, 81
*Creative Confidence* (Kelley and Kelley), 56, 106
*Creative Habit, The* (Tharp), 101, 107
*Creativity* (Csikszentmihalyi), 53
creativity: and definitions of "smart," 6, 32; ego and fear as inhibiting, 32, 45; and future business trends, 3, 4, 22, 154; Humility as fostering, 67; impediments to, natural and cultural, 4, 5, 23, 28; and Managing Self, 98, 105, 107; and mindfulness practice, 84, 88–89; mistakes/failures as opportunities for, 51–53, 55–56, 178; open-mindedness as key to, 49; at Pixar, 175–78; team approach to, 4, 31; tools for, 101
*Creativity Inc.* (Catmull), 71–72, 175
*Critical Thinking* (Paul and Elder), 39
critical thinking: defined, 24; and definitions of "smart," 32; and future business trends, 3, 22; Humility as fostering, 60, 63, 67; identifying with one's beliefs, 39–46; impediments to, natural and cultural, 4–5, 23, 24–27; and mindfulness practice, 84; open-mindedness as key to, 49–50; team approach to, 4, 60, 110, 126; tools for, 100, 102–4. *See also* thinking
Csikszentmihalyi, Mihaly, 53

## D

Dalio, Ray, 7, 46–47, 70, 85–86, 89–90, 107, 131
Davidson, Richard, 106
Deci, Edward L., 162
Dennett, Daniel, 29

*Dialogue: The Art of Thinking Together* (Isaacs), 117
Dutton, Jane, 91, 124–25
Dweck, Carol, 54–55, 64

**E**
Eastern philosophy, 8, 48, 63, 85
economic impact of technology, 2–4, 18–20, 154
Edison, Thomas, 28, 52
Edmondson, Amy, 166
ego: "big me" culture, 60–61, 68; and emotional intelligence, 112–13; fear and, as learning inhibitors, 7, 11, 32, 37, 45, 47, 105; identifying with one's beliefs, 39–46; and mediocrity principle, 65–66, 90; NewSmart
ego (*cont.*) Organization as mitigating, 11, 155, 156, 169, 179; and perfectionism, 54; and positive self-talk, 108–9; and Reflective Listening, 116–18. *See also* Humility; Quieting Ego
Ehrenreich, Barbara, 93
Elder, Linda, 26, 39–40, 42, 45, 50
emotional engagement (SMA Skill): and definitions of "smart," 32, 38; and future business trends, 3, 22, 154; Humility as fostering, 7, 65; impediments to, natural and cultural, 4–5, 23; as team oriented, 60
emotional intelligence (EI), 110–14, 170
emotions: cognition as intertwined with, 4, 26–27, 105, 106; gratitude, practice of, 92–93; management of, 105–10, 138; and mindfulness practice, 81, 82, 84–85, 89, 105; positive emotions in work environment, 160–61; sensitivity to, 110–14. *See also* fear
Ericsson, Anders, 143
evolutionary biology, 4, 24–25, 28–29, 105
*Explaining Creativity* (Sawyer), 101
*Extreme Ownership*, 72

**F**
Facebook, 20, 163
failure: learning from, 6, 28–29, 51–56, 173, 178; permission to fail, 166, 172, 173, 174, 177–78
fear: ego and, as learning inhibitors, 7, 11, 32, 37, 45, 47, 105; innovation as stifled by, 159, 160; management of, 107–8; of mistakes and failure, 28–29, 52–53, 179; NewSmart Organization as mitigating, 11, 155, 156, 166–68, 169, 175–76, 179; and Quieting Ego, 79, 92
fight-flee-or-freeze response, 4, 28–29, 95, 105
Firestein, Stuart, 48
Ford, Martin, 20

Fredrickson, Barbara, 5, 77–78, 123, 160

**G**
Gardner, Howard, 20
gender differences, 111–12, 170
Gilbert, Daniel, 80
*Give and Take* (Grant), 69
giving (generosity), as tied to success, 69
Gollwitzer, Peter, 109
Google: AlphaGo, 17, 21, 171; and employment trends, 20; Humility as mindset at, 8, 71, 171–72; hyperlearning environment of, 171–75; organizational system of, 158, 169, 170, 183
Grant, Adam, 69, 166
gratitude, practice of, 92–93
Greek philosophy, 38, 47, 48, 63, 64

**H**
*Handbook on Character Strengths and Virtues* (Peterson and Seligman), 49
Hassabis, Dennis, 17
Healy, Alice, 143
Horniman, Alec, 130
*Humans Are Underrated* (Colvin), 31
*Humble Consulting* (Schein), 129
*Humble Inquiry* (Schein), 118–19
Humility: defined, 7–8, 59–60; and emotional intelligence, 112, 113; and gratitude, 92; as hero of SMA story, 8–9, 187; intellectual tradition of, 63–64; and Managing Self, 67, 96; misperceptions of, 60–62; organizations with mindset of, 8, 69–72, 171–72, 177; and Otherness, 127; and perfectionism, 53; psychology of, 64–68; and Quieting Ego, 67, 79, 89; Reflection Time questions, 66, 73; and Reflective Listening, 67, 116–17
hyperlearning, defined, 159

**I**
IBM, 16, 17, 20, 21
*Iconoclast* (Berns), 108
IDEO, 56, 101, 107, 158, 183
if-then implementation plans, 109–10
ignorance (not knowing), embrace of, 46–51, 70, 84, 119, 157
*Ignorance: How It Drives Science* (Firestein), 48
*Immunity to Change* (Kegan and Lahey), 148
income inequality, 2
Industrial Revolution: jobs lost to technology in, 3; learning not a priority in, 21; mental models from, 6, 31, 33, 35; and organizational systems, 157; transformative nature of, 1, 18, 19
*Inevitable, The* (Kelly), 19

innovation: and definitions of "smart," 6, 32; fear as biggest inhibitor of, 159, 160; and future business trends, 3, 21, 22, 52, 154–55; at Google, 171–75; Humility as fostering, 67, 68, 69, 70–71; impediments to, natural and cultural, 4, 5, 23, 27–28; and Managing Self, 98; and mindfulness practice, 81, 83, 84, 88–89; mistakes/failures as opportunities for, 51–52, 55–56, 173; open-mindedness as key to, 49; team approach to, 4, 27, 31, 60, 110, 115, 126, 170
intelligence. *See* artificial intelligence; emotional intelligence; NewSmart
Intuit, 8, 52–53, 70–71, 101, 158, 179
*Intuition Pumps and Other Tools for Thinking* (Dennett), 29
Isaacs, William, 117–18, 119
Isen, Alice, 160

**J**

James, William, 80–81
Johnson, Steven, 51–52
Jourard, Sidney, 125, 128

**K**

Kabat-Zinn, Jon, 80, 81, 82, 84, 86, 87
Kahneman, Daniel, 24–26, 43, 48, 100, 102
Kaplan, Jerry, 12
Kegan, Robert, 148–49
Kelley, David, 56, 107
Kelley, Tom, 56, 107
Kelly, Kevin, 19
Killingsworth, Matthew, 80
Klein, Gary, 100, 101–2
knowledge workers, 2–3, 18, 22, 31–33, 119
Kross, Ethan, 109

**L**

Lahey, Lisa Laskow, 148–49
leadership: and future business trends, 154–55; at Google, 71, 172–73; and Humility, 69–72; at Pixar, 71–72, 177; and Reflective Listening, 121; role modeling of behaviors, 159, 167–68, 180–81; and Self-Determination Theory, 163–65; and small-team structures, 170; and stress-testing of business models, 98; training of managers, as insufficient, 23
learning: ego and fear as inhibiting, 7, 11, 32, 37, 45, 47, 105; at Google, 171–75; Humility as fostering, 8, 63–65, 177; hyperlearning, defined, 159; as iterative or continuous, 6, 20–21, 28, 32, 51, 154, 155, 177; listening as essential to, 117; mistakes/failures as opportunities for, 6, 28–29, 51–56, 173, 178;

and organizational systems, 155, 157, 170; at Pixar, 175–78
*Learn or Die* (Hess), 46–47, 162
Lehman, Darrin, 63–64
Liedtka, Jeanne, 101, 130
listening. *See* Reflective Listening

**M**

management, workplace. *See* leadership
Managing Self, 95–114; Assessment Tool for, 136–38; benefits of, 95–96; and emotional intelligence, 110–14; emotions, management of, 105–10, 138; and Humility, 67, 96; Reflection Time questions, 99, 110, 114; relation of, to other NewSmart Behaviors, 76, 78, 123–24; slowing down, practice of, 96–97; thinking, management of, 97–104, 136–37
*Marshmallow Test, The* (Mischel), 76, 109–10
Maslow, Abraham, 156
Mayer, J. D., 110–11, 112
McKinsey & Company, 19, 22
mediocrity principle, 65–66, 90
*Mindset* (Dweck), 54
*Mindfulness* (Penman), 82–83
*Mindfulness for Beginners* (Kabat-Zinn), 86–87
mindfulness: meditation in practice, 81–82, 85–90; and "meta-emotions," 105; and positive self-talk, 109; principles and benefits of, 80–85; and Reflective Listening, 117, 145
Mischel, Walter, 76, 107, 109–10
modesty vs. humility, 68
Myers, P. Z., 65–66

**N**

Neff, Kristin, 61
NewSmart, 35–57; as hero of SMA story, 8–9, 187; identifying with quality, not content, of beliefs, 39–46; ignorance (not knowing), embrace of, 46–51; and Managing Self, 97; measurement criteria for, 6–7, 36–37; mistakes/failures as learning opportunities, 51–56; outdated mentality, dangers of, 35–36; principles of, listed, 38; vs. quantity-based definitions of "smart," 6–7, 31–33; Reflection Time questions, 42, 44, 50, 57
NewSmart Behaviors, overview of, 5, 9–10, 33, 75–78. *See also* Managing Self; Otherness; Quieting Ego; Reflective Listening
NewSmart Behaviors Assessment Tool, 133–49; introduction to, 10, 133–34; for Managing Self, 136–38; for Otherness, 140–41; for Quieting Ego, 135–36; for Reflective Listening, 139–40; using results of, 142–49

NewSmart Organization, 153–86; Assessment Tool for, 183–86; emotional competencies as key to, 159–60, 169–70; future business trends, listed, 153–55; Google's hyperlearning environment, 171–75; Pixar's hyperlearning environment, 175–78; positive emotions, power of, 160–61; processes, importance of, 179–81; psychological foundations of, listed, 11, 156; Psychological Safety in, 166–68; Reflection Time questions, 161, 164, 165, 167; and Self-Determination Theory, 162–65; technology as humanizing force in, 10, 156–58

Ng, Andrew, 19

*No Humans Need Apply* (Kaplan), 12

**O**

Oettingen, Gabrielle, 109

Old Smart: ego's investment in, 38, 40, 43, 123; mistakes/failures not tolerated in, 6, 52, 53, 55, 56; vs. NewSmart, 44, 46, 51, 56; organizations modeled on, 157; as quantity based, 6, 31–33

*Originals: How Non-Conformists Move the World* (Grant), 166

Otherness (emotionally connecting to others), 123–31; Assessment Tool for, 140–41; Dutton's keys to, 124–25; Humility as fostering, 67, 127; and language choices, 130–31; Reflection Time questions, 124, 130; relation of, to other NewSmart Behaviors, 76, 78, 123–24; workplace relations, 125–29

**P**

Pagel, Mark, 49

Paul, Richard, 26, 39–40, 42, 45, 50

Penman, Mark, 49

perfectionism, 53–55

Pixar: Humility as mindset at, 8, 71–72; hyperlearning environment of, 175–78; and identifying with one's beliefs, 44–45; and NewSmart's genesis, 7, 39; organizational system of, 158, 169, 170, 183

positive self-talk, 108–9

positivity, 11, 156, 160–61, 169, 179

*Positivity* (Frederickson), 77–78

Powell, Lili, 86

PreMortem tool (Klein), 101–2

*Principles of Psychology* (James), 80–81

psychological distancing, 107

Psychological Safety, 11, 156, 166–68, 169, 172–74, 175, 177, 179

**Q**

Quieting Ego, 79–93; Assessment Tool for, 135–36; daily reminders for, 90–92; gratitude, practice of, 92–93; and Humility, 67, 79, 89; inner talk, negative aspects of, 79–80; mindfulness meditation in practice, 81–82, 85–90; mindfulness principles and benefits, 80–85; Reflection Time questions, 83, 86, 90, 93; and Reflective Listening, 116–18; relation of, to other NewSmart Behaviors, 76, 78, 123–24

Quinn, Jim, 70

**R**

rationality, 26–27

Reflection Time, guidelines for, 34

Reflective Listening, 115–22; asking vs. telling, 118–20; Assessment Tool for, 139–40; Assessment Tool results, building on, 144–45, 148–49; checklist for, 120–21; Humility as fostering, 67, 116–17; importance of, 115–16; and NewSmart Organization, 157; and Quieting Ego, 116–18; Reflection Time questions, 118, 119, 122; relation of, to other NewSmart Behaviors, 76, 78, 123–24

reframing of negative situations, 107–8

*Rise of the Robots* (Ford), 20

robot apocalypse, fears of, 15, 17

root cause analysis, 100

Roth, Bernard, 108, 131

Rovelli, Carlo, 49

Ryan, Richard, 162

**S**

Salovey, Peter, 110–11, 112

Sawyer, R. Keith, 101

Schein, Edgar, 118–19, 129

scientific method, 38, 46, 48–51, 173–74, 176

Self-Determination Theory, 11, 156, 162–65, 169, 174, 176–77, 179

self-regulation. *See* Managing Self

Simon, Herbert, 26, 180–81

slowing down, practice of, 96–97

Smart Machine Age (SMA), 15–34; economic impact of, 2–4, 18–20, 154; humanness as blessing and curse in, 23–29; Humility as key to success in, 7–9, 60, 72 (*see also* Humility); vs. Industrial Revolution, 1, 3, 18, 19, 21; inward vs. outward focus in, 29–31; jobs left to humans in, 3, 21–23, 31, 154–55; machines' increasing autonomy and intelligence, 2–3, 15–18, 171, 188; mental models for, 33–34; personal career implications of, 1–2, 4, 11–12; Reflection Time questions, 34; "smart" as defined in, 6–7, 31–33, 36–37 (*see also* NewSmart); as team oriented, 4, 60, 110, 112, 126, 158, 170

SMA Skills: collaboration as key to, 28, 31, 114; and future business trends, 3–4, 21–23, 31, 153–55; Humility as fostering, 7, 65, 66–67, 72; impediments to, natural and cultural, 4–5, 23–29; listed, 3, 22; NewSmart Behaviors as fundamental to, 5, 9, 33, 75–78, 120; NewSmart ideals as fostering, 31–32, 56–57; and openness to new information, 29–31; and organizational excellence, 159, 179–81; and Reflective Listening, 115, 119; and scientific thinking, 48; and slowing down, 96; and stress-testing of beliefs, 130

Smith, Brad, 70

Socrates, 47, 48, 63, 64

stress-testing of beliefs, 21, 37, 66, 67, 98, 102, 130–31

System 1 vs. System 2 thinking, 24–26, 96, 98, 117

**T**

Tangey, June Price, 65

Tanzi, Rudy, 108

technology: advances in, as transformative, 2–3, 15–18, 171, 188; economic impact of, 2–4, 18–20, 154; as humanizing the work environment, 10, 156–58; jobs left to humans due to, 3, 21–23, 31, 154–55

Tegmark, Max, 49

Tharp, Twyla, 101, 107

*Thinking, Fast and Slow* (Kahneman), 24, 43, 48

thinking: critical thinking, defined, 24; in dichotomies, 131; emotions as intertwined with, 4, 26–27, 105, 106; and evolutionary biology, 4, 24–25, 28–29, 105; Humility as

fostering, 60, 63, 67; identifying with one's beliefs, 39–46; management of, 97–104, 136–37; and mindfulness practice, 80–90; not knowing, being good at, 46–51, 70, 84, 119, 157; openness to new information, 29–31, 41, 46, 49–51, 116–18; processing speed, 118; scientific method, 38, 46, 48–51, 173–74, 176; speed of cognitive processing, 118; System 1 vs. System 2, 24–26, 96, 98, 117; team approach to, 4, 60, 110, 126. *See also* learning

*Train Your Mind for Peak Performance* (Bourne and Healy), 143

*Transparent Self, The* (Jourard), 125

Tweed, Roger, 63–64

**U**

US military, 8, 72, 100–101, 158, 161, 183

**W**

Waal, Frans de, 66

Wagner, Tony, 20

Wallace, Amy, 45

Watson supercomputer, 16, 21

*Where Good Ideas Come From* (Johnson), 51

Wiener, Norbert, 15, 17

Williams, Mark, 82–84, 87

Willingham, Daniel, 24

workers: autonomy of, 162–64, 172; contingent workers, rise of, 2, 20; and income inequality, 2; jobs lost to technology, 3–4, 18–20; jobs that will survive SMA, 3, 21–23, 31, 154–55; knowledge workers, 2–3, 18, 22, 31–33, 119

*Work Rules! Insights from Inside Google …* (Bock), 71, 173

World Economic Forum, 22

# About the Authors

Ed Hess is professor of business administration and Batten Executive-in-Residence at the University of Virginia, Darden School of Business. He focuses on teaching, researching, writing, and consulting in organizational learning, growth/innovation cultures, leadership, behaviors, and processes.

Katherine Ludwig, a former corporate finance and securities lawyer, is a research, editing, and publishing associate at the University of Virginia, Darden School of Business.

## Berrett–Koehler
## Publishers

**Berrett-Koehler** is an independent publisher dedicated to an ambitious mission: Connecting people and ideas to create a world that works for all.

We believe that the solutions to the world's problems will come from all of us, working at all levels: in our organizations, in our society, and in our own lives. Our BK Business books help people make their organizations more humane, democratic, diverse, and effective (we don't think there's any contradiction there). Our BK Currents books offer pathways to creating a more just, equitable, and sustainable society. Our BK Life books help people create positive change in their lives and align their personal practices with their aspirations for a better world.

All of our books are designed to bring people seeking positive change together around the ideas that empower them to see and shape the world in a new way.

And we strive to practice what we preach. At the core of our approach is Stewardship, a deep sense of responsibility to administer the company for the benefit of all of our stakeholder groups including authors, customers, employees, investors, service providers, and the communities and environment around us. Everything we do is built around this and our other key values of quality, partnership, inclusion, and sustainability.

This is why we are both a B-Corporation and a California Benefit Corporation—a certification and a for-profit legal status that require us to adhere to the highest standards for corporate, social, and environmental performance.

We are grateful to our readers, authors, and other friends of the company who consider themselves to be part of the BK Community. We hope that you, too, will join us in our mission.

**A BK Business Book**

We hope you enjoy this BK Business book. BK Business books pioneer new leadership and management practices and socially responsible approaches to business. They are designed to provide you with groundbreaking and practical tools to transform your work and organizations while upholding the triple bottom line of people, planet, and profits. High-five!

To find out more, visit **www.bkconnection.com**.

# Berrett–Koehler
# Publishers

Connecting people and ideas
to create a world that works for all

Dear Reader,

Thank you for picking up this book and joining our worldwide community of Berrett-Koehler readers. We share ideas that bring positive change into people's lives, organizations, and society.

**To welcome you, we'd like to offer you a free e-book.** You can pick from among twelve of our bestselling books by entering the promotional code **BKP92E** here: http://www.bkconnection.com/welcome.

When you claim your free e-book, we'll also send you a copy of our e-news-letter, the *BK Communiqué*. Although you're free to unsubscribe, there are many benefits to sticking around. In every issue of our newsletter you'll find

- A free e-book
- Tips from famous authors
- Discounts on spotlight titles
- Hilarious insider publishing news
- A chance to win a prize for answering a riddle

Best of all, our readers tell us, "Your newsletter is the only one I actually read." So claim your gift today, and please stay in touch!

Sincerely,

Charlotte Ashlock
Steward of the BK Website

Questions? Comments? Contact me at bkcommunity@bkpub.com.

MIX
Paper from
responsible sources
FSC® C011935
www.fsc.org

Certified

Corporation
bcorporation.net